The Witches Almanac

Spring 2025—Spring 2026

CONTAINING pictorial and explicit delineations of the
magical phases of the Moon together with information about astrological
portents of the year to come and various aspects of occult knowledge
enabling all who read to improve their lives in the old manner.

The Witches' Almanac, Ltd.

Publishers   Providence, Rhode Island
www.TheWitchesAlmanac.com

Address all inquiries and information to
THE WITCHES' ALMANAC, LTD.
P.O. Box 25239
Providence, RI   02905-7700

13-ISBN: 978-1-938918-95-7 The Witches' Almanac—Classic Edition
13-ISBN: 978-1-938918-94-0 The Witches' Almanac—Standard Edition
E-Book 13-ISBN: 978-1-938918-93-3 The Witches' Almanac—Standard Edition
Español 13-ISBN: 978-1-938918-92-6 The Witches' Almanac—Standard Edition

ISSN: 1522-3184

First Printing July 2024

Printed in USA

Established 1971 by Elizabeth Pepper

Preface

We arrive once more at the threshold of a new edition of *The Witches' Almanac*. As the seasons turn and the stars dance, we find ourselves drawn to a theme that has been as constant and enduring as the cosmos itself—Trust. Trust is the thread that weaves the fabric of community. In an age of uncertainty, it is trust that anchors our souls and acknowledges our relationships with others.

Trust in **Oneself** is one of the first steps on the path of the Wise. To gaze into the mirror of truth and see not only what is, but what could be, requires a steadfast heart and a fearless spirit. Our spells and rituals are simply reflections of our inner strength, our will made manifest in the physical realm. Trust that your intentions, both pure and true, will shape the world as the potter shapes the clay. Honor Ptah.

Trust in our **Ancestors** and the ancient knowledge they bestowed to us. Each herb, each incantation, each talisman, and every invocation carry with it the weight of centuries, a testament to our enduring Craft. Honor the Mighty Dead.

Trust in the **Natural World**. The earth beneath our feet, the sky above and the waters that flow are not mere elements, but sacred allies. In every rustling leaf and whispering breeze, there is a promise—a bond of mutual respect and understanding. To walk the path of the Witch is to walk in harmony with nature, to trust in its cycles and recognize its gifts. Honor Cernunnos.

Finally, trust in the **Community** of seekers and practitioners. We are not solitary stars, but constellations. In these pages you will find shared journeys, each a collection of spirit and forged connections that transcend the mundane. Honor Ma'at.

As you embark on another year of discovery and enchantment, let trust be your guiding star. Whether you are a seasoned practitioner or a novice, may the knowledge within these pages illuminate your path and fortify your spirit.

HOLIDAYS

Spring 2025 to Spring 2026

March 20, 2025 . . . . Vernal Equinox
April 1 . . . . All Fools' Day
April 30 . . . . Walpurgis Night
May 1 . . . . Beltane
May 8 . . . . White Lotus Day
May 12 . . . . Vesak Day
May 29 . . . . Oak Apple Day
June 5 . . . . Night of the Watchers
June 20 . . . . Summer Solstice
June 24 . . . . Midsummer
July 23 . . . . Ancient Egyptian New Year
July 31 . . . . Lughnassad Eve
August 1 . . . . Lammas
August 13 . . . . Diana's Day
August 17 . . . . Black Cat Appreciation Day
August 27 . . . . Ganesh Chaturthi
September 22 . . . . Autumnal Equinox
October 31 . . . . Samhain Eve
November 1 . . . . Hallowmas
November 16 . . . . Hecate Night
December 16 . . . . Fairy Queen Eve
December 17 . . . . Saturnalia
December 21 . . . . Winter Solstice
January 9, 2025 . . . . Feast of Janus
February 1 . . . . Oimelc Eve
February 2 . . . . Candlemas
February 15 . . . . Lupercalia
February 17 . . . . Chinese New Year
March 1 . . . . Matronalia
March 19 . . . . Minerva's Day

Astrologer . . . . Dikki-Jo Mullen

Climatologist . . . . Tom C. Lang

Cover Art and Design. . . . Kathryn Sky-Peck

Sales . . . . Roy Singleton

Bookkeeping . . . . D. Lamoureux

Fulfillment . . . . Casey M.

ANDREW THEITIC
Executive Editor

GWION VRAN
Art Director

MAB BORDEN
Copy Editor

CONTENTS

C O N T E N T S

The Life of an Almanac Through Time

IN A WORLD driven by technology and instant information, the almanac stands as a timeless treasure that has endured for centuries. But what exactly is an almanac?

Modern almanacs trace their roots back to ancient civilizations with some of the earliest examples dating back to the Babylonians, the Egyptians and beyond. Originally, they may have served as astronomical and agricultural guides, providing crucial information on celestial events, tides and seasonal cycles. As the wheel of time turned, the almanac evolved to encompass a vast range of topics, including weather forecasts, historical events, medical advice and even recipes.

The true essence of the almanac lies in its ability to encapsulate a wealth of information within its pages. It combines astronomy, astrology, meteorology and folklore, delivering a diverse array of knowledge. Readers can delve into predictions for the astrological Sun Signs, eclipses, lunar phases and cycles, Solstices and Equinoxes, alongside planting charts and weather forecasts. From Moon phases to tide tables, from farming advice to historical anniversaries, an almanac covers a wide spectrum of subjects, making it a multifaceted companion for curious minds seeking wisdom across various realms. And, in our case, a treasure-trove of information for the Witch and Magician alike—be sure to check out our Sunrise/Sunset tables when calculating your planetary hours!

In an era when digital tools dominate, the tactile experience of flipping through the pages of an almanac evokes nostalgia and connects us to centuries-old practices. It serves as a tangible reminder of our connection to the natural world, preserving knowledge and traditions that might otherwise fade away.

While the prevalence of digital resources has diminished the prominence of physical almanacs, they continue to find a place in our modern lives. Many almanacs now exist in digital formats, ensuring their accessibility and expanding their reach. But, despite these adaptations, their essence remains the same—an almanac is a compendium that encapsulates a year's worth of knowledge, inviting readers to explore the world around them. We, at The Witches' Almanac, in addition to providing a digital format for Witches on the go, have chosen to continue the old way of printing a paper almanac as well, knowing that the touch provides more magic.

—THEITIC

Yesterday, Today and Tomorrow

by Timi Chasen

OTHERWORLDLY The many-worlds interpretation (MWI) of quantum mechanics, which posits the existence of countless parallel universes for every quantum event, is increasingly influential in the realm of magical thought and practice. This interpretation aligns with magical perspectives that consider multiple possibilities and realities, enhancing the conceptual overlap between quantum physics and metaphysics.

In magic, the MWI provides a theoretical foundation that resonates with the idea of alternative realities and the potential of intentions to influence outcomes. Practitioners may see their spells and rituals as techniques to navigate or sway these parallel realities, aiming to select paths that correspond with their desired results. This approach conceptualizes magical practices as a form of quantum manipulation, where focused intent and ritualistic actions are viewed as means to transition between possible worlds.

This integration of quantum mechanics into magical practice not only enriches the theoretical underpinnings of magical phenomena but also encourages a fusion of scientific and magical paradigms. It prompts practitioners to delve into more complex metaphysical theories and experimental approaches, merging cutting-edge scientific concepts with traditional magical practices. As quantum theories like the MWI continue to develop, they are set to further influence and expand the scope of how magic is understood and practiced in contemporary settings.

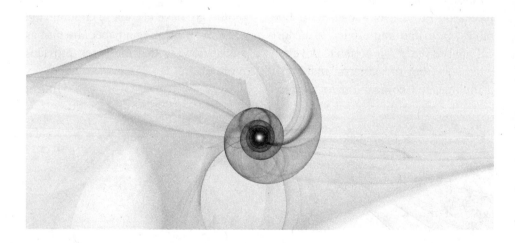

GOULISH GARDEN The Mowing Devil story, originating from a 1678 pamphlet titled *The Mowing-Devil: or, Strange NEWS out of Hartford-shire,* presents a fascinating early account of what might be considered a crop circle. This narrative unfolds in Hertfordshire, England, where a farmer, frustrated with a laborer's high wage demands for mowing his field, exclaimed that he would prefer even the Devil to do the work instead. According to the legend, that very night, an eerie glow fire-like enveloped the field, captivating and alarming the local residents. By morning, the field was perfectly mowed with such remark-able precision that it seemed beyond human capability, suggesting a supernatural influence.

This legend encapsulates how humans historically have sought to explain and attribute meaning to unusual natural phenomena, viewing them through the lens of their cultural and spiritual beliefs. It serves as an early example of the kind of stories that predate and possibly presage modern interpretations of crop circles frequently associated with otherworldly or mystical origins. The Mowing Devil story has evolved over time, integrating with contemporary folklore and mythology that embrace a broad spectrum of supernatural and alternative explanations for such events. This account continues to intrigue and resonate, offering a glimpse into the interplay between human perception, nature's mysteries, and the supernatural, highlighting the enduring fascination of the unexplained.

WINTER'S DREAM The Cailleach, a venerable figure deeply woven into Celtic mythology, stands as an embodiment of the harshness of Winter and the elemental power of the land. Her presence is particularly significant during Imbolc, a traditional Gaelic festival that heralds the onset of Spring. Celebrated on February 1, Imbolc Eve is a time of weather divination, and the behavior of the Cailleach during this festival is keenly observed for signs of the season ahead.

According to folklore, the Cailleach is a Winter deity who governs the weather and the environment. As Imbolc approaches, it is said that she makes a decision that will determine the length and severity of the remaining Winter. If the Cailleach wishes to prolong the cold and barren season, she chooses Imbolc as the day to gather her firewood. This is because she needs ample wood to sustain herself through extended Winter weeks. Therefore, a bright and clear Imbolc day is seen as an omen that Winter will continue well beyond its expected course, as the clear weather allows the Cailleach to collect plenty of wood.

On the other hand, if the Cailleach deems that Winter should recede and give way to Spring, she does not need to collect much wood. Consequently, she allows the weather on Imbolc to be dark, wet, and dreary, signaling that she has no need to stock up for a longer Winter. This tradition underlines her dual role not only as a harbinger of Winter's ferocity but also as a guardian who ensures the timely arrival of Spring. The dreary weather on Imbolc thus brings hope, suggesting that warmer, fertile days are near as the Cailleach retreats, allowing life to flourish anew.

This mythology beautifully illustrates the Cailleach's significance in Celtic lore as a custodian of seasonal balance and transformation. Her actions during Imbolc remind the people of the cyclic nature of

life and the continuous interplay between destruction and renewal. Through her, the myths convey messages about endurance, change, and the delicate balance of nature. As a figure who navigates between the realms of the earthly and the divine, the Cailleach during Imbolc embodies the profound connection between human communities and the mystical forces that govern their world.

WITCH WAY UP Witch stairs, also known as alternate tread stairs or space-saving stairs, are a distinctive type of staircase designed to maximize the use of limited space in smaller homes or buildings. These stairs are characterized by alternating treads, where each step extends only halfway across the stair width, resulting in a staircase that is steeper and more compact than conventional ones. This clever design allows the staircase to fit into narrower spaces, efficiently connecting floors without occupying extensive horizontal area.

The term "Witch stairs" is richly rooted in folklore, imbuing these structures with an aura of mystery. According to legend, these stairs were believed to deter Witches, who were thought to be thwarted by the irregular pattern of the steps. This belief reflects the superstitions of historical times, where such nuances in everyday structures were often linked to protective measures against supernatural forces. While there is no historical evidence to confirm that these stairs were purposefully built to ward off Witches, the lore surrounding them contributes an intriguing layer to their architectural history.

Found primarily in older buildings, particularly those from colonial periods, Witch stairs are a testament to the ingenuity of past builders who needed to optimize limited space. Today, these stairs not only serve a functional purpose but also capture the imagination, offering a glimpse into the cultural and architectural practices of earlier times.

www.TheWitchesAlmanac.com

Author Bios

Meet New Contributors

Darien Rae   Rebecca Halladay

Loren Crawford   Amelia Ingram

Jan Fry   Shani Oates

Nina Falaise   Clair Pingel

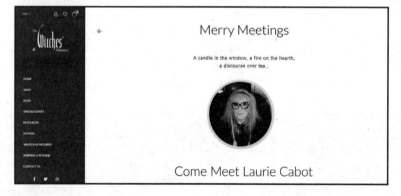

Merry Meetings

A candle in the window, a fire on the hearth,
a discourse over tea...

Come Meet Laurie Cabot

Come visit us at the
Witches' Almanac website

News from The Witches' Almanac

Glad tidings from the staff

At this time of year, we see our dedicated efforts blossom into the latest edition of *The Witches' Almanac*. This work is a heartfelt tribute to our craft, born from a commitment to seeking old and new ways that change the magical landscape and inform our interaction with the world. Our mission extends beyond mere compilation—it fosters an environment where diverse perspectives enlighten, challenge and inspire. We embrace the ongoing evolution of magic and mysticism, recognizing that giving these voices space to be heard is both an honor and a duty. By doing so, we ensure the dialogue within our community remains vibrant and relevant.

This year, our chosen theme is "Air: Breath of the Cosmos." What better way to understand the essence of life than through the words and thoughts that flow like the wind, connecting us all? As we stand on the threshold of tomorrow, we persist and strive for a deeper connection, not only for ourselves but for the entire world. The breath of the cosmos inspires us to reach new heights and embrace the boundless potential within and around us.

We are excited to announce the release of *Ancient Holidays*, a new book series exploring the spiritual calendars of ancient civilizations. The first three books by Mab Borden, covering the Egyptians, Greeks and Romans, have arrived and been warmly received. As we finish this year's Almanac, we are beginning work on the fourth book in the series. Additionally, *Celtic Tree Magic* is being reimagined by Rachel Nagengast. Her depth of knowledge is creating a tome that will inform even the seasoned Celtic devotee, available before the end of the year.

In *The Witches' Almanac Issue 44*, we present an exciting collection of brilliant minds, featuring a mix of familiar and up-and-coming thinkers. We warmly welcome Darien Rae, Loren Crawford, Jan Fry, Nina Falaise, Rebecca Halladay, Amelia Ingram, Shani Oates and Clair Pingel to our pages. We are thrilled to announce the second edition of the Almanac translated into Spanish, introducing a new logo for our Spanish edition! Additionally, we proudly introduce the *2025 Witches' Almanac Wall Calendar* centered around the theme of symbols from around the world. As always, you can anticipate captivating imagery and concise explanations of each symbol.

We strive to enhance your experience at TheWitchesAlmanac.com, our online store and Pagan resource center. We are currently working on expanding our inventory of collectible items, which can be found at TheWitchesAlmanac.com/pages/collectibles The *50 Year Anniversary Edition of The Witches' Almanac* and *Magic: An Occult Primer—50 Year Anniversary Edition* are highly favored by our shoppers. These items have become must-haves and remain in high demand. Will there be reprints? Only time will tell!

TIME AND THE SACRED YEW

TIME means nothing to the Yew. This tree is apparently immortal, with a lifespan of thousands of years. Immortality being one of the attributes of a God, the tree's longevity is one of the reasons ancient cultures such as the Egyptian and Hittite regarded it as a deity. Little surprise, then, that Goddesses such as Ningishzida and Inanna were associated with yews and may even have been the trees themselves! These deities were known as triple Goddesses of Life, Death and Eternity. In the Norse culture, humans were believed to have been born from trees and after Ragnarok—the end of the world—it is expected that they will be born from them again.

For a long time, there was speculation as to which species of tree the Tree of Life actually was and doubt as to whether it was a real tree at all! However, this tree was absolutely central to the ancient Egyptians, who kept it in the temple of Heliopolis and whose main obsession was with immortality, which they went to great lengths to achieve. However, by the time of the pyramids the Egyptians were depicting it as various unlikely trees such as the short-lived sycamore or palm.

The Yew is the One—not any old yew but *Taxus sanctus*, the Sacred Yew. This precious tree was brought to Britain as dry staffs to be planted in remote sanctuaries for safe keeping into the distant future. This practice of bringing yew staffs to Britain from such places as the Holy Lands, the Caucasus and Armenia went back thousands of years and was still going on in the early Christian period. One of the Celtic saints, St. Padarn, was given a staff by the Archbishop of Jerusalem. It is likely that he planted it over his daughter's grave where it grew into the most extraordinary-looking yew tree at Llanerfyl in mid Wales. This yew consists of four trunks that wind and weave horizontally around the churchyard, looking like giant serpents—but then the Tree of Life has always been connected with serpents. Remember the Garden of Eden and the apple tree? Well, they weren't ordinary apples. They were apples of immortality, as the red yew fruits were known. This was the tree named in Medieval times as "the tree of the thrice-blessed fruit"— the acorn which the fruit resembles in its early stages of development, the nut which is deadly poisonous, the kernel and the apple which is the red flesh called the *aril*, the only part of the tree which is not toxic. Indeed, you can eat the fruits which are sweet as grapes, but make sure you don't swallow the nut or pip. It's not a pleasant death.

The Yew was sacred to all cultures of the Northern hemisphere at one time. In Japan, a creation myth told of the Gods arriving by sky boat to the Holy Mountain where the yews already grew and then merging with them, cloaking themselves with Yew. To this day, the Emperor carries a yew staff as a symbol of his divine authority, made from the wood of these trees.

So what message do these sacred trees carry for modern people? They are so much older and wiser than any person living. They are sentient beings who know what it was like on Earth before humanity came and messed the place up. The trees' DNA is as nature intended in a world where so much is genetically modified to suit the needs of human beings. The world is increasingly manmade, although humans don't have the knowledge—never mind the wisdom—to know what changes will be ultimately beneficial. Humanity doesn't really know who it is or where it came from. Modern people may even be a kind of hybrid between Gods and humans but are only just beginning to understand the planet Earth, its environment and climate, the life forms who share it, and the context in which all exist. Modern humans are only just learning how to fit with it all and recognizing the need to make space for other species to survive.

On first look at the Tree of Life, it's obvious it's got things right. Unchanged in 200 million years, it has been watching humanity and wants for nothing but humans to come to their senses. The ancient DNA it carries means the Yew knows how things were meant to be and what humanity needs to do if it is to continue here on Earth. People change everything to what they think might be better for themselves and then find they've got it wrong because they haven't taken into account the web of life which supports them and everything else on Earth. This is what the Tree of Life knows and it could teach so much if a person just sat in silence for a while

beneath a sacred Yew and listened. It could take you back to humanity's origins, speak to you about where people went wrong sometime around the Industrial Revolution, about the need to curb human appetites for more and more of everything—particularly fossil fuels, plastics and addictive junk food. All this is making humans and the environment sick.

Sitting under a Yew can take you time travelling. People have gone back in time with a Yew in a quiet churchyard. Sometimes it's important to take time out in order to move forward. Sometimes you have to experience the Underworld, protected like Aeneas by a golden bough , that magical talisman written about by the Roman poet Virgil.

Yews are so massive, complex, magical and mysterious that you can hardly fail to feel awed in their presence. They have stood there as humanity evolved and changed the face of the Earth. Just for their great age alone— some over 5,000 years old—they command respect, yet they have no legal protection and these ancient ones are still being lost. For those interested, there is a petition on change. org Campaign for Legal Protection for Ancient Yews, which stands at over 318,000 signatures. Yews have been here for such a very long time, yet modern humans have only existed for 300,000 years! Yews have seen and know a lot more than people.

—JANIS FRY

16

HORSE WHISPERING
Legendary Tactics of Mastery

THE SOCIETY of the Horseman's Word was founded in the nineteenth century for the most practical of purposes. In a faltering Scottish economy, large land-owners were buying up hardscrabble little farms which depended on sturdy draft horses as basic work units. Novices hired out as plowmen, trainers and black-smiths, undercutting the wages of the skilled. The experienced workers—to protect themselves and their beloved animals—formed the organization and offered a whiff of magic. People called the members "horse Witches" and believed that they knew a secret word that could calm unruly, frightened or suffering animals. Like the Masons—an older trade league with its own mystique—elaborate rituals sprang up around the Horseman's Word.

Initiation, meetings

The induction ceremony offers plenty of melodrama, including elements of solemnity, fright and fun. Aspirants are summoned to a candlelit barn between eleven p.m. and one a.m. and blindfolded at the door. Usually plowboys, they kneel and form a circle, left feet bare and hands raised. A mock minister stands within the ring and vows them to absolute secrecy, verbal or written, about the proceedings.

They learn that Cain was the first Horseman and that certain verses of the Bible read backwards can summon the Devil for aid. The backward pages forward events—a stench of sulphur and banging noises signal the arrival of the Devil. The terrified novices are told to shake hands with the Evil One and find themselves clutching a cold, wet hoof. When the "minister" removes the blindfolds, a hideous figure is revealed in animal skins and a horned mask. The cere-mony could have been a travesty of what farmers believed were Witches' sabbats, developed from information derived from folklore or published accounts of earlier Witch trials.

As is likely for attendance at any Scottish occasion, whiskey turns up at initiations, this time with bread as a sacrament. So braced and sanctified, the aspirants learn the Society's secret ritu-als—Masonic-style gestures, handshakes, passwords. Then each one hears in his own ear a whisper of the Word said to master any horse. At regular membership meetings, the Scotch flowed freely and you can imagine that good horsey stories flowed as well in the nature of shoptalk (*e.g., a few years ago in East Anglia, there was this crazy Clydesdale mare and....*)

Say what?

Now as then, people are wildly curious about the historical magic word. A gibberish sound, cadabra? An obvious word, calm? Only Horse Whisperer and horse know for sure. The whisperer keeps his secret—the famous Clever Hans himself never achieved speech or he might have made a deal for behaving (give sugar.)

There is one lucky clue that wheels the tale around in a dizzying direction. One source claims that in the rich farming area of East Anglia the magic consists of two Latin words, sic iubio, "thus I command." The language implies that the Romans brought the technique to Britain during its four centuries of occupation. Horse whispering may be far more ancient than we realize—Rome was the most extreme of historical horse cultures. The animals played a major role in the military and the roaring public's favorite sport, chariot races.

Horse sense

Flora Thompson, depicting nineteenth century Oxfordshire in *From Lark Rise to Candleford*, provides an explanation from a noted horse whisperer. According to observers, the village blacksmith calmed fearful horses by touching their manes and whispering into their ears. Asked about horse lingo, Matthew replied, "I only speak to 'em in their own language." As he banged horseshoe to hoof, that was the extent of his explanation.

The Horse Whisperers played out their heyday during the 1870s, a power in rural life throughout Britain. Highly respected for their mastery, horsemen who possessed the Word were given the best jobs. Their influence continued until the 1930s when farm machinery and trucks rumbled into place, impervious to communication. Horse whispering still exists here and there in remote places. Robert Redford's 1998 film, *The Horse Whisperer*, renewed interest in the practice and the terminology floats around the blogosphere here and there. Sometimes the posting requests photos or a phone conversation with the animal, offers usually evoking derisive comments.

Skills and scams

To get jobs in earlier times, unscrupulous workers figured out how to prove their own whispering skill. They slyly provoked animals and then controlled them in a number of ways familiar to trainers.

Putting tacks under collar or saddle made for crazy behavior, but was too easy to detect. Often the horse's keen sense of smell aided and abetted in gaming the system Exposing the animal to certain obnoxious substances, for instance, would cause him to balk. As the outraged horse refused to budge, the trickster claimed supernatural power, the basis for the old "horse Witch" claim. The scam was called "jading." A variety of organic substances served the purpose, sometimes hidden on or near the horse, sometimes smeared on the forehead of the alleged Witch. They included liver from stoats or rabbits, dried and powdered with "dragon's blood," vernacular for a red resin from a palm fruit. Certain oils—cinnamon, rosemary, fennel—caused balking or escalated frenzy. Mischief achieved, the deceiver whispered into the horse's ear, the language a secret between human and horse. Now the soothing "magic" came into play with the animal's behavior. Horsemen knew that they could draw a horse toward them with some sweet-smelling tidbit, especially effective in taming the wild. Once approached, the trainer slipped the horse hidden crumbs of fragrant cake or gingerbread, the munching a giant step toward control.

Toadmen amulets

Tricksters made use of two amulets to aid in jading or drawing. On the tongue of a newborn foal, alongside the cheek, lay a substance called milt. No one knew what the fibrous matter was all about, but they had traditionally retrieved it to carry. Horsemen also secured a particular bone from a frog—possessors of this talisman were believed to be warlocks. The bone was shaped like a wishbone and sometimes the bone of a toad was substituted. In either case its owner was known as a Toadman.

Properly prepared, the little bone fitted the horned V-shape called a "frog" on the underside of a horse's hoof—visual and verbal imitative magic. But the bone required ritual attention before it could be nailed to the frog on the hoof or carried by the horseman. The killed frog or toad was hung on a whitethorn bush for twenty-four hours to dry and placed in an anthill for a month. The skeleton was flung into a stream at the Full Moon and the horseman watched until a little center section floated on the current. The remaining piece closed to form a V, the desired amulet.

Sometimes the powder was mixed with jading substances to repel. Sometimes the bone might be kept whole, cured with jading materials, wrapped in linen and hidden on the horseman. A touch on the shoulder jaded the horse, a touch on the rump drew the horse. An impressive performance, enhancing the legendary skill of horse whisperers and perhaps sleight of hand illusionists.

—BARBARA STACY

Mystic Verses and Cosmic Whispers

Exploring the World of Islamic Magic

WITHIN ISLAM, the the concept of magic encompasses a broad spectrum of beliefs and traditions, reflecting the diverse and intricate cultures that adopt them. These practices trace their origins to ancient times. Spanning millennia, they date back to the *Jahiliyyah* period—also known as the period of ignorance—which preceded the emergence of Islamic history in the Arabian Peninsula. Encompassing various facets of daily life, these traditions intertwine the ordinary with the spiritual, bridging the gap between the visible and unseen realms.

Before Islam became the dominant faith in Arabia, the prevailing religious beliefs centered around a multitude of Gods and Goddesses, each associated with different aspects of nature and life. Prominent among these were Al-Lat, Al-Uzza and Manat, often revered together as a trio and worshipped in temples and shrines throughout the region. Alongside these major deities were numerous local spirits and entities—including the *Jinn*—which held a significant place in Arabian spiritual cosmology.

The concept of Jinn in particular is deeply rooted in pre-Islamic Arabian culture, with these beings believed to inhabit remote areas like deserts and ruins and to be capable of influencing human affairs. To safeguard against their perceived capriciousness, people employed amulets, charms and rituals as protective measures, a tradition that later influenced Islamic magical practices.

Evil Eye amulets hanging in front of building

explicitly acknowledging their existence and portraying them as beings created from smokeless fire. This recognition facilitated the continuation of pre-Islamic practices associated with Jinn, albeit within the context of Islam. The tradition of utilizing amulets and talismans—now often adorned with Quranic verses or the names of Allah—can be traced back to similar pre-Islamic customs aimed at warding off harm or malevolent spirits.

The influence of pre-Islamic supernatural beliefs is evident in contemporary Islamic folk magic customs which persist in various regions of the Muslim world, particularly among rural communities and those closely connected to traditional ways. Despite being adapted to Islamic contexts, practices such as healing rituals, protective charms and divination retain traces of their pre-Islamic origins. For example, the utilization of specific herbs, incantations and rituals for averting the evil eye or treating illnesses draws upon ancient magical traditions predating Islam.

Additionally, the ongoing reverence for local saints and revered figures in certain Islamic societies mirrors pre-Islamic customs of honoring significant individuals or ancestors. These figures are believed to possess *barakah* (divine grace) and are thought to intercede on behalf of individuals—a concept that, while integrated into Islamic theology, reflects older practices of seeking assistance from spiritual intermediaries.

Additionally, animism and totemism were prevalent belief systems, attributing spiritual essence to animals, plants and even inanimate objects. This worldview fostered a rich tradition of magical rituals aimed at harnessing the inherent powers of the natural world.

Following the emergence of Islam in the seventh century, the Arabian Peninsula underwent a profound shift as Islamic monotheism gradually supplanted the polytheistic and animistic beliefs of the Jahiliyyah era. However, rather than completely discarding these pre-Islamic beliefs, Islam incorporated and reinterpreted many aspects of them within its own theological framework. For instance, the belief in Jinn was integrated into Islamic theology, with the Quran

Origins and Evolution

The evolution of Islamic magic is deeply rooted in the spiritual landscape of pre-Islamic Arabia where diverse practices flourished among the Arab peoples. With the advent of Islam in the seventh century, these ancient traditions underwent a transformative process, integrating into the fabric of Islamic belief while retaining echoes of their polytheistic past. This fusion gave rise to a diverse array of magical traditions, blending Islamic teachings with local customs and drawing inspiration from the broader tapestry of ancient Near Eastern and Mediterranean magical practices. This manifests in myriad cultural forms catering to both practical and spiritual needs across diverse communities, some of which are listed below:

Talismans and Amulets: Among the most recognizable artifacts of Islamic magic is the *Hamsa* or Hand of Fatima, a palm-shaped amulet widely believed to ward off the malevolent influence of the evil eye. Symbolic objects like these serve as conduits for spiritual protection, embodying the intricate interplay between faith and symbolism in Islamic magic.

Poetry and Scripture: The expressive medium of poetry has long been intertwined with Islamic mysticism, offering a vehicle for conveying esoteric concepts and spiritual insights. When coupled with verses from the Quran, poetry becomes a potent tool in protective rituals and healing practices, underscoring the profound reverence for scripture within Islamic magical traditions.

Planetary Influence: The legacy of ancient civilizations' fascination with celestial bodies endures in Islamic magic through the practice of Astrology. Despite its contentious nature, Astrology reflects humanity's enduring quest to comprehend and harmonize with the cosmic forces believed to shape individual destinies.

Supernatural Beings: Central to Islamic cosmology and magical practices are the enigmatic Jinn, beings crafted from smokeless fire with the capacity for both mischief and benevolence. The rituals aimed at appeasing or harnessing their powers exemplify the intricate relationship between humans and supernatural entities in Islamic magic.

Throughout ages and across lands, a shared conviction persists in the potency of spiritual practices to influence the tangible realm and safeguard against unseen threats. Whether through the invocation of Quranic verses for protection, the crafting of intricate talismans for warding off harm or the observance of auspicious celestial alignments for pivotal endeavors, Islamic magic reflects a universal human

Talismanic prayer scroll.

A hamsa protection pendant.

yearning for transcendence and the solace found in ritual and symbol.

Poetry and word as magic

In Islamic tradition, poetry and the profound utterances found in ancient texts stand where language transcends mere communication to become a vessel for spiritual insight and transformation. This mystical dimension of words—deeply rooted in Arab and Islamic intellectual heritage—is revered for its ability to connect the human soul with the divine, harness esoteric knowledge and invoke spiritual realities. The magical use of poetry draws upon both pre-Islamic practices and the rich legacy of Islamic mysticism and highlights a belief in the inherent power of articulate expression to influence the unseen world, offering protection, healing and a means to attain deeper states of consciousness.

The legacy of poetry and ancient writings as sources of magic and wisdom predates the advent of Islam—pre-Islamic Arab culture was rich in oral traditions and lyrical expressions imbued with power and mystery. These ancient practices survived the transition into Islamic times, merging seamlessly with the new religious and cultural paradigm. Poetic verses laden with symbolic and allegorical content continued to be seen as possessing an innate power capable of affecting the fabric of reality. Within this context, poetry serves not just as artistic expression but as a sacred act, with recitations believed to have the capacity to ward off evil, attract blessings and facilitate communion with the divine.

Today, the reverence for poetry and the mystical use of words retain their significance in Islamic culture, reflecting a continuous thread of spiritual practice that spans centuries. The enduring belief in the transformative potential of poetry and ancient texts underscores a broader appreciation for the depth and potency of language. As carriers of ancient wisdom and magical potency, these words bridge the past and present, offering insights into the human condition and the perpetual quest for understanding and connection with the greater cosmos. In this way, poetry and the written word remain not only a testament to the rich spiritual heritage of Islam but also a living tradition that continues to inspire and elevate.

Talismans and the Hamsa

Talismans have long been objects of fascination and utility across various cultures, revered for their supposed magical properties to protect, heal or bring fortune to their bearers. These objects are often crafted with specific symbols, inscriptions or materials and are believed to possess mystical powers. They serve as physical manifestations of the human desire for control over the uncertainties of life. The use of talismans transcends religious and cultural boundaries, illustrating a universal aspect of human belief in the supernatural.

A prime example of a talisman that has achieved widespread recognition and use is the Hamsa. Known also as the Hand of Fatima in Islamic cultures, the Hamsa is a palm-shaped amulet popular throughout the Middle East, North Africa and beyond. It typically features an open right hand, sometimes with an eye depicted in its center. It is believed to ward off the evil eye—an ancient curse thought to be cast by a malevolent glare causing misfortune or injury. The Hamsa represents a synthesis of cultural beliefs, embodying protection against harm and invoking blessings for its owner.

The appeal of the Hamsa lies not only in its protective function but also in its artistic and cultural significance. It has been adopted and adapted by various religious and cultural groups, each imbuing the symbol with its own meanings and aesthetic variations. In Islamic tradition, the Hamsa is often associated with the daughter of the Prophet Muhammad—Fatima Zahra—and symbolizes patience, faith and loyalty. This layering of symbolism adds depth to the talisman's protective qualities, linking it to revered historical and spiritual figures.

Talismans like the Hamsa demonstrate the enduring belief in the power of symbols to influence the spiritual and material realms. They are tangible expressions of hope, faith and the complex interplay between humanity and the unseen forces of the universe. As objects of cultural exchange and adaptation, talismans also highlight the shared human experiences and beliefs that transcend individual traditions, uniting people across different faiths and backgrounds in their common quest for protection and blessing.

The enigmatic world of Jinn

As supernatural entities within Islamic theology, Jinn stand at the intersection of pre-Islamic beliefs and Islamic cosmology. Originally ancient Arabian spirits of nature or local deities, Jinn were seamlessly integrated into Islamic thought and acknowledged as beings created by Allah from smokeless fire. This evolution from pre-Islamic to Islamic beliefs highlights the adaptability and continuity of religious and cultural practices, showing how Islam embraced and redefined existing traditions.

Within the broad spectrum of Muslim culture, Jinn are known to possess free will, allowing them to choose paths of good or evil, similarly to humans. This capacity for moral choice positions them as figures of both fear and fascination, capable of acts of kindness or malice or of displaying neutrality. Stories and folklore rich with encounters involving Jinn reflect the imaginative depth and cultural diversity of Islamic societies. These tales emphasize Jinns' unpredictable nature, shape-shifting abilities and movement through unseen realms.

The role of Jinn in daily life and spiritual practices also varies widely across cultures, with some communities invoking them for protection, assistance in love or vengeance despite orthodox prohibitions. These practices blend Islamic beliefs with ancient traditions and highlight the syncretism present in many Muslim societies. Celebrated in literature and pop culture—notably in *One Thousand and One Nights*—Jinn continue to intrigue and inspire, connecting ancient lore with modern fascination. This enduring interest in Jinn not only adds to the richness of Islamic cultural heritage but also encourages deeper contemplation of the unseen aspects of the divine creation.

Planetary Magic

The belief in planetary influences is a fascinating aspect of Islamic magic that intertwines ancient astrological knowledge with Islamic spiritual practices. This concept, while somewhat contentious within the strictest interpretations of Islamic theology, has historically found a place in the broader cultural and esoteric traditions of the Muslim world. It reflects a nuanced understanding of the cosmos in which celestial bodies are not merely inert entities floating in space but are imbued with significance and power that can affect human lives and the natural world.

At the heart of this belief is the idea that each planet, along with the Sun and Moon, exerts a unique influence on Earth and its inhabitants. This influence can manifest in various aspects of life, including personality traits, life events and even the health of individuals and communities. Astrologers—often well-versed in both Islamic scholarship and ancient astronomic texts—would create detailed charts to map out these influences based on the positions of celestial bodies at specific times. These charts could then be used to determine the most auspicious moments for undertaking important tasks, making significant decisions or initiating new ventures.

In addition to their role in divination and decision making, planetary influences were also thought to intersect with the practice of creating talismans and amulets. Certain verses from the Quran, names of Allah or symbols associated with specific planets would be inscribed on these objects during auspicious alignments to harness the protective or beneficial energies of those celestial bodies. This practice illustrates the sophisticated integration of astrological knowledge with Islamic spirituality, aiming to draw upon the divine blessings mediated through the cosmos.

Looking back, Islamic magic has deep roots in pre-Islamic Arabia. These ancient beliefs merged with Islam, giving rise to a whole range of magical practices. From talismans like the Hamsa believed to ward off evil to the mystical power of poetry and scripture and even the influence of celestial bodies like planets, Islamic magic reflects a blend of old and new, practical and spiritual.

In the end, Islamic magic reminds you of the shared human desire to connect with something bigger than yourself. Whether it's reciting verses for protection, carrying a lucky charm or looking to the stars for guidance, these practices offer comfort and hope across cultures and time. They speak to the timeless quest for meaning and the power of belief to shape our lives.

—DEVON STRONG

THE SCORN POLE:

Níðingr, Skimmity and Riding the Stang

IN MEDIEVAL Scandinavia, reputation was everything. Being the object of shame and humiliation was ruinous—so much so, in fact, that a man could rightfully challenge slanderers to a duel and even kill them. A person unable or unwilling to defend their honour from shaming barbs of spite was a social pariah. The visitation of spite upon a person in the form of a curse was referred to as *níð* (*nith,*) imprecating scorn and ridicule. In Anglo-Norse society, the scorned miscreant was thusly dubbed as *níðingr* (*nithing.*) Referring specifically to traits deemed to be unmanly, the terminology relates to the social stigma attached to a coward or a person of loose morals. Also on this list of people considered to be social deviants were male practitioners of sorcery, wife-beaters and, conversely, hen-pecked and cuckolded husbands.

Punishment was swift and visceral. The reviled person was exposed and subjected to defamation and ridicule—often through a very public tongue lashing (*tunguníð* literally means "níð of the tongue")—a ritual poetic scolding pronounced against violators of social mores and contracts. It was believed that only the most severe rebuking would break any spells that afflicted the níðingr which forced them to act against their true nature. It was a verbal exorcism of sorts. A more demonstrative procedure known as tréníð (literally, carved níð, meaning "wood-shame") involved a hazel pole, a *níðstang*—the scorn pole.

Once recognised for their abhorrent behaviour, transgressors had their dastardly deeds publicly exposed through a riotous procedure involving the níðstang or níþing pole. Use of the níðstang or scorn pole is attested in the old Icelandic law book, *The Landnámabók* (Book of Settlements,) though it seems to have been a long-established form of social justice before it was recorded there. The níðstang possibly evolved from very crude carvings whose purpose was to mock or curse. Rudolf Simek describes these as, "*wooden poles with carved human faces in order to curse particular people, in which the intention was probably less to curse than to mock the person.*" A long hazel pole was selected to become an effigy of the person to be shamed. One end of the pole was crudely carved to resemble human features. The pole or stang was then paraded about, accompanied by a cacophony of discordant banging and clattering intended to drive away the malefic spirit affecting the despicable wretch, while humiliating them for their inappropriate behaviour and for acts committed under its spell.

Scorn and ridicule were the antithesis of the Germanic ethic in which honour and status meant everything—a man was less than nothing without them. Redress for any attack on a man's honour was the obligation of his existence. However, it could only be sought in truth. Lies and falsehood could not be defended. There were complex rules surrounding the restoration of reputation. Moreover, the procedure under the law was expensive. As a sacred, legal force, lawcourts were the preserve of the privileged only. Anyone of unequal status could even the odds in a *hólmganga* (duel,) using the force of arms and the calling of Otherworldly spirits to hone the outcome against an opponent who could not be defeated any other way. Brief descriptions of this procedure appear in numerous folk sagas and lays in which feuding men settled bitter arguments in a duel to satisfy honour. Hólmganga challenges were a lawful way to draw swords against another man, avoiding potential murder charges and wergild payments.

Failure to attend allowed the person insulted to shout three *níðings* (curses)

at the person who'd caused them offense. The carefully delineated hólmganga (duelling) arena was known as the *hólmgangustadr*, a sacralised, bounded area—commonly a *hólm* (island) or a three-way crossroad. Part of the sanctification process required four *höslur* (hazel posts) to mark the corners of the nine-foot square inner arena allotted for combat. When everything was ready, the square was said to be "*völlr haslaðr*" (hazelled.) Given that hazel is also the wood specified for the níðstang, there is an apparent significance in the choice of wood that relates to Otherworldly justice, an imposition of the highest court. In fact, the same ritual procedure created the *frið-garð* (law-courts.)

During the Viking Age, the níðstang was often the final recourse open to those of limited means. The early fourteenth century Icelandic *Vatnsdæla Saga* records an incident set four centuries earlier where inflammatory insults fuelled the need for a duel to restore honour. Finbogi failed to show up for the hólmganga, forcing Jökul to raise a níðing pole against him for his unmanly cowardice. Jökul killed a mare and laid its head and flayed carcass over a hazel pole around nine feet in length, onto which he'd carved crude human features and a rúnic curse along the top edge of his selected hazel pole. Jökul expounds vitriolic contempt for Finbogi's cowardice. The níð bars him from the camaraderie and fellowship of all good men, making him an *útlagi* (outlaw,) condemned to live as *skogarmaor* (man of the forest,) damned as a truce breaker under the wrath of the Gods. In extreme cases, the man was exiled, losing all the privileges of life, denied all rights to succour and shelter from kith and kin.

A níðstang scorn pole is basically a powerful animal totem created to accompany as the vehicle for a níð, the curse itself. The pole was erected in a public place to maximise the shame—it was meant to be seen. It was theatre at its most dramatic and deadly. Primarily, the níðstang was intended to disrupt and unsettle the *landvættir* (land-wights) inhabiting the ground where the cursed person's dwelling stood. These spirits would in turn vent their curses upon the targeted person whose livelihood and life would thereafter be destroyed.

Níðstangs were used in this way to desecrate swathes of land in a technique known as *alfreka* (literally, "driving away of the elves")—an extreme measure that effectively destroys the fecundity of the land and the beneficent relationship between the landvættir and its inhabitants who depend upon them for their survival. As fierce protectors of their native lands, the landvættir are intolerant of mistreatment and dishonour. Harmony is essential for prosperity. Maintaining that relationship requires considerable sensitivity, a caution reflected in the first clause of settlement law in Iceland, circa 930 CE,

which states that no one may approach the island in ships sporting horrifying dragon-head prows. Any ship furnished with them must remove or cover them to avoid intimidating the landvættir. Moreover, the efficacy of such a device is clearly evident in the carved horse-head gables of countless modern houses in parts of Germany and Scandinavia.

Most notorious of all níðstang events is that enacted by Egil in the thirteenth century Icelandic saga named for him, again set much earlier, circa ninth to tenth century. Embroiled in a bitter conflict with the Norwegian King Eiríkr and Queen Gunnhilðr over swindled inheritance, status and land (a disagreement that resulted in murder and the corresponding rights for wergild,) Egil Skallagrímsson erected a níðstang on the island of Herdla, directing it towards his enemies on Norway's mainland. A mare's head was placed on a hazel pole on which he'd carved his runic curse. Egil erected his níðstang and while invoking his curse against Eiríkr and Gunnhilðr, he turned the horse's head towards the mainland, calling upon the guardian-spirits who dwell there to wander without rest until Eiríkr and Gunnhilðr were driven out of the land.

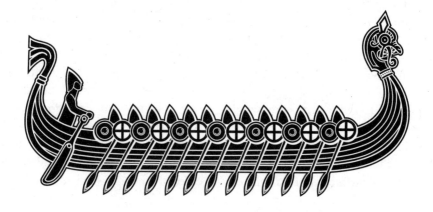

Egil's níðstang shares the same core elements as Jokul's. The author of this saga leaves the reader in no doubt that the curse—rather than any desire for public shaming—is the most significant factor here. The procedure is simple enough: the skill resides in mastery of runes in the construction of the níð, erected on a remote spot away from the gaze of would-be spectators. As a skald of great renown and a sorcerer of Sámi descent, Egil conducts numerous magical acts throughout this and other sagas that feature him. Essentially rendering the entire mainland as *hólmgangustaðir*, Egil's níð coerces the landvættir into judging Eiríkr and Gunnhilðr in order to cast them out as outlaws.

Níðstangs remained in situ only until retribution or recompense is felt to have occurred. The pole may then be taken down and destroyed. Egil Skallagrímsson's saga recounts that the effects of his níðstang curse were soon evident—Eiríkr and his Gunnhilðr were forced to flee to the British Isles.

Increased secularisation and changes to the law ultimately led to the abandonment in Iceland of the hólmganga ritual, removing direct appeals to sacred law, the old law of the land, and so the sagas that recollect these customs are unable to properly convey the relationship between the landvættir, law and the people. In later centuries, níðstangs were raised against any man deemed to be guilty of any type of anti-social behaviour. Public scorning was imposed upon those guilty of drunkenness and lewd behaviour, behaviours warranting shame. If the crime was deemed heinous enough, a

peripatetic procedure known as "riding the stang" was called for—an activity that demonstrates the trend towards a more personal and hands-on approach in the visitation of a níð. Rough justice became the only manner of address open to the poor and those without power or authority.

Nevertheless, in later centuries, the deep social stigma attached to various acts of unmanly behaviour by which a man was deemed to have lost his honour was undiminished. Street justice prevailed against all charges of behaviour considered outside the societal norms, which almost always attached to unmanly conduct. Acts of public shaming and scorning customs continued unabated for wife-beaters, drunkards, cowards and sexual deviants or those of loose morals, etc., in a rough justice procedure known as "putting a man on the stang" or the "skimmity ride" in popular parlance. The now-widespread English folk custom of riding the stang has a variant in the West Country known as "the skimmington ride" or "rantanning."

Medieval transgressors were dragged from their homes, beaten with sticks, thrown onto níðstangs or nithing poles (a board or gate eventually replaced the pole used in earlier centuries) and carried around the village, exposing them to abusive verbiage designed to bring public shame for their lack of honour. Others rang bells, rattled bones and banged old pots and pans with sticks as the men recited a mocking doggerel rhyme called a "nominee" after the Latin benediction, "in nomine Patris." There is even an account of riding the stang in the diaries of Samuel Pepys—a writer famous for his social commentaries—dated June 10, 1667. Apparently, while in Greenwich he witnessed the town's constable humiliated for allowing his wife to beat him. Riding the stang became illegal in 1882 but persisted nonetheless. Punishments of this nature for moral laxity appear in Thomas Hardy's *The Mayor of Casterbridge*. Hardy's novels are a feast for lovers of folk tradition.

Similar European traditions arose as charivari—troops of masked musicians who patrolled the streets creating havoc and mayhem as they meted out vigilante punishments guaranteed to bring humiliation and embarrassment to alleged perpetrators. The victim could even be displayed upon a donkey in person or as an effigy. The "crimes" were the subject of mime, were exhibited as bawdy theatrical performances or were exclaimed as a litany of obscenities and insults. Charivari migrated to the US and Canada where it became known as shivaree or chivaree, respectively. This performance was recognised as a method of maintaining a moral boundary through the public humiliation of people who failed to act according to proprieties of social law. Punishments were meted widely and loudly for adultery and illegitimacy—in fact, for any and all acts deemed to violate public decency or appropriate behaviour.

During later centuries of public unrest, rising poverty and tremendous social injustice, the charivari processions became heavily politicised. Recognised by the disenfranchised, they became a platform to give voice to protestations of injustice and inequality. Leading figures in government and town councils were subject to polemical attacks, either directly on their person or through the use of wooden effigies that were beaten and burned in their name. Charivari became ritualised in its unrelenting subversions. Scorn and mockery were demonstrated in acts of inversion in which pigs, goats and donkeys were ridden backwards by the persons being lampooned. Clothing worn by the charivari revellers was inside-out or back to front. Gender identities were swapped and music was discordant—all actions designed to exaggerate the social disorder the performers felt was generating disruption of the norm. Justice could only be sought if it was first made known and public declarations left no doubt of that.

—SHANI OATES

The Scratch of a Demon

IN THE DOMAIN of human existence there lies a bloody battle that often goes unseen. It is the struggle against our inner demons—those intangible forces that gnaw and scratch at our souls, consuming us from within, bit by bloody bit. Most of us have experienced it. Some of us nearly died of it. Many have.

One layer of this battle is the denial of certain aspects of ourselves. This type of suppression can morph into a festered wound, poisoning our minds and distorting reality. The weight can become unbearable, the boulder too heavy to carry. These wounds need release or they will slowly suppurate into a blackened rot of self-destruction and sorrow.

The scratch of a demon is difficult to heal. Mending requires plunging into a realm where contradictions intertwine and paradoxes flourish. Here, light inter-

mingles with darkness, passion entwines with apathy and courage coexists with fear. The very essence of our being becomes fragmented as we grapple with these perplexing dualities—embodying both hero and villain and saint and sinner simultaneously. It is a disorientating dance of chaos and uncertainty that demands a willingness to embrace discomfort as we confront those unsavory parts of ourselves deemed unworthy or unacceptable. Yet it is precisely through this confrontation that true transformation can occur.

By stepping into these uncharted territories, we gain access to a wellspring of untapped potential, a source from which liberation, strength and redemption emerge. It is within the black that we unearth hidden reserves of fortitude—the kind that emanates from acknowledging our vulnerability rather than denying it. Navigating the depths of the subconscious requires patience and perseverance. It involves an unwavering commitment to untangling the nuanced web woven by years of conditioning.

I have roamed the landscape of internal battlefields with phantoms relentlessly gnawing at my sanity, painting images without the color of hope. The strokes between truth and illusion were blurred, leaving me in a state of perpetual woe, searching for the cause of this ongoing melee. It is a twisted piece of performance art in which dancers are fragments of the fractured psyche, their lines distorted and their intentions obscured.

I have always carried a darkness within, its origin an accumulation of disquieting questions. What catalyzed the birth of this shadowed entity? Is it an intrinsic part of me? Was it nurtured by external influences or did it arise from some innate aspect of my being? Is it the reconciliation of past-life karma? Imprisonment as payment for debts of the past? *What do you want with me?*

Over time this darkness began to consume me. Shadows danced with eerie grace, mocking me with their elusive forms. They flickered across every surface of my life, distorting familiar shapes into grotesque caricatures that tormented my senses. My mind became a maze where reason faltered and doubt reigned supreme. I roamed its winding passages, desperately seeking solace amidst the fire of emotions that engulfed me. These emotions surged with an intensity that defied comprehension. They manifested in unexpected ways, arising from the darkest recesses of my mind. This energy became its own living entity—an inadvertent tulpa sewn into the cloth of my daily life, dictating my actions and cloaking my dreams. It was an untamed wildfire raging across dry plains, consuming everything in its path with a voracious hunger for release. It created chaos where there was once harmony and sowed doubt where there was once certainty. My love waned as my mind turned to shade.

These battles are not fought solely in isolation—they spill over into every facet of existence. Moments meant for joy become tainted by the specter of doubt lurking just beneath the surface. Relationships falter beneath the weight of mistrust bred by internal struggle. And the guilt, a forever scar.

As I grew older, the weight of these demons bore me down into hell. Their relentless grip tightened around my throat, constricting my breath until it felt as though I was suffocating under their presence.

"What am I supposed to do with this?" was all I could ask myself.

This darkness with its insidious influence can consume us entirely if left unchecked. Only by confronting it and finding our light can we hope to regain control. It took me years to acknowledge the reflection in the mirror. But there came a time when an undeniable magnetism drew me to stop, turn and stare.

In this moment I saw darkness and light entwined in a dance of enigmatic allure. I was beckoned to engage and challenge the boundaries of belief and the provocation of uncertainty. I stepped into the fringe where my logic and reason faltered. My mind became entangled in a web spun by ambiguity with no clear answers or defined paths. My tower crumbled. I had to rebuild and forge a new path.

At first I felt destroyed, my flesh ripped apart, cooked and eaten by the ghoulish thoughtforms I created so long ago to survive and escape. My survival tactics had become a jumbled mishmash of elemental imbalance, creating the destruction that almost brought me to my end. My creativity had been hijacked by a storm of elusive caricatures and I needed to change the story.

I was the only one who could break through this thicket. When I assumed sole responsibility for my emotions, actions, thoughts and creativity, I found the strength that led me out of the confines of torture machines and blood baths and into a matrix that would shed light into my darkness. I found that the very parts I was suppressing were the parts that empowered me. They were not liabilities—they were embers of Power *and I took them back.*

In these times when it feels as though life has been reduced to mere ashes and smoldering ruins, it is precisely then that we discover our inner strengths—the dormant embers waiting to be stoked back to life. Redemption comes in various forms. The answer is finding ways that resonate and work for the individual. For me, holding the hands of my inner ghouls quiets the storm enough to notice their gifts. Examining their hands and tracing the lines exposes their individual essence. By learning their language, I am better able to discern the pain they carry to find the healing they need. I also find more answers in the small as opposed to the large. Oftentimes it starts with smaller changes to meet our current needs and then builds from there. Before long we will look back and notice the vast ground we have covered.

Reconciling the neglected parts of ourselves is a dark journey, but one that is necessary if inner peace is desired, and for magic to flourish. This journey is necessary to rectify those things that are destined and connected to this incarnation. It is a journey that is possible through self-awareness and action.

This trek may not fully resolve the deepest parts of our hearts but it will forge the tools necessary for transformation on a new level. It provides the strength to fight with courage and vigor. It gives us the ability to harness our power and create with tempered vision. After all, it is we who are creating every moment of our lives. The sooner we acknowledge the magnitude and impact this has upon our realities, the sooner we can utilize our deepest powers and potentialities that will unlock the doors of everything and anything we considered impossible or unreachable. By espousing accountability and facing our demons head on, we can gain control once again. The pea under the mattress will begin to dissolve. And no matter how daunting a task it seems, we possess the strength and capacity for redemption within us. We must believe in ourselves and believe in our aptitude for creating the life we strongly desire. *Own your Power.*

—DARIEN RAE

THE WILD HUNTSMAN

THY rest was deep at the slumberer's hour
If thou didst not hear the blast
Of the savage horn, from the mountain-tower,
As the Wild Night-Huntsman pass'd,
And the roar of the stormy chase went by,
Through the dark unquiet sky! The stag sprung up
   from his mossy bed
When he caught the piercing sounds,
And the oak-boughs crash'd to his antler'd head
As he flew from the viewless hounds;
And the falcon soar'd from her craggy height,
Away through the rushing night!
The banner shook on its ancient hold,
And the pine in its desert-place,
As the cloud and tempest onward roll'd
With the din of the trampling race;
And the glens were fill'd with the
   laugh and shout,
And the bugle, ringing out!

From the chieftain's hand the wine-cup fell,
At the castle's festive board,
And a sudden pause came o'er the swell
Of the harp's triumphal chord;
And the Minnesinger's thrilling lay
In the hall died fast away.

The convent's chanted rite was stay'd,
And the hermit dropp'd his beads,
And a trembling ran through the forest-shade,
At the neigh of the phantom steeds,
And the church-bells peal'd to the rocking blast
As the Wild Night-Huntsman pass'd.

The storm hath swept with the chase away,
There is stillness in the sky,
But the mother looks on her son to-day,
With a troubled heart and eye,
And the maiden's brow hath a shade of care
Midst the gleam of her golden hair!

The Rhine flows bright, but its waves ere long
Must hear a voice of war,
And a clash of spears our hills among,
And a trumpet from afar;
And the brave on a bloody turf must lie,
For the Huntsman hath gone by!

—MRS. FELICIA DOROTHEA BROWNE HEMANS, 1793-1835

The Trickiest Toad

IN COLOMBIA, we know that toads are not honest things. Our people remember many tales, much mischief from toads. They are smart and don't care for anyone, although it is not true about warts, toads do not do those little things that look like their own skins. The trickiest toad of all lived long ago, many grandfathers, but we still tell his stories over the campfires. In this happening I will tell, a famous race Toad won from Deer, we believe it is so.

One day Toad said to Deer, "Let's you and me have a race to see which is faster."

Deer made a rasping sound, a Deer laugh. "Don't be silly, Floppy Legs," he said."You couldn't run as fast as me. Why would I want to waste my time dashing around for no reason? I only put on speed when I smell hungry hunters."

"Oh, let's race just for a little fun around here," said Toad. "Also I will bet a bag of gold just to make it worthwhile for you, my friend."

"Oh, well, why not take such easy money?" said Deer. "After three days I will meet you here and show you who runs the fastest, Sticky Tongue."

At dawn on the day of the race, Toad met with his fellow creatures, all pushing, shoving and croaking with excitement. He persuaded them to stay hidden all along the stretch of the road. "When you hear Deer approach," Tricky Toad told them,

say, "What took you so long? Here I am ahead of you." Meanwhile, I will return to the finish line and we will see who wins this race, for a race is not always to the swiftest."

At the appointed hour Deer trotted into the starting line and greeted Not-So-Tricky-Toad as his challenger, for everyone knows all toads look alike. They set off, Deer in an easy lope, a pleasant outing on a fine morning.

After awhile he asked, "Where are you, Toad?" And another relay toad further down the road answered from a distance, "Here I am, ahead of you."

"He is ahead of me! Incredible!" said the fastest of the forest creatures, picking up his pace in a way serious.

Further along Deer asked again, "Where are you, Toad?" And again he heard from a different toad, "Here I am, ahead of you."

"This is ridiculous," said Deer, by now panting. "I can't let Toad win the race. How could I explain

such a result? My whole herd will be disgraced."

Deer ran faster than ever, but he was past his strength even before he reached the finish line, where Toad already crouched.

"I give up," Deer gasped. "I will never race you again."

Since that time, our people have never heard of such a race.

—BARBARA STACY

Adapted from a Bogota folk tale

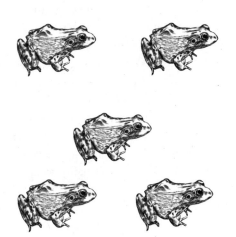

The Witch

THE 2015 FILM The Witch is a masterpiece. Roger Eggers, the writer, producer and director of the film indicates that he wishes the film to be taken literally. The story is derived from folklore and journals of the period. The setting takes place in New England in the 1630s and circles around a Puritan family. It is billed as a horror story and is a brilliantly written and acted epic, centering on the literal interpretations of conviction and devotion. Each character is an examination of layers of both faith and belief and the manifestations derived from these embodiments—which is the true horror in the film.

It is important to note that the Puritans believed their purpose in life was to attain righteousness so that they would be with their God in the afterlife. Within their communities the men with the most wealth were perceived as the most righteous—therefore, they became the most powerful and served as the governors and magistrates as well as preachers. Subsequently, if anything went wrong within their communities, i.e., crops failing, illness or the death of a child, there were only two explanations. The first was that the community or individuals within the community were not righteous enough and their God was angry and punishing them, or secondly, it was the work of the Devil. The Witch, by Puritan standards, was the concubine of the Devil.

The story opens with William, the patriarch of the family, standing before the Church Elders as they are in the process of excommunicating him from the settlement. The Elders approach William with the opportunity to back away from his stance so they do not have to excommunicate him and his family, as they would have to leave as well. William responds to the Elders with, "I cannot be judged by false Christians." It is apparent that the reason for William's excommunication is his self righteousness and that the Elders were truly attempting to talk him down from his position. His wife Katherine stands by him stoically while the Elders pass down their judgment. There is notable fear on the expression of their children's faces. Fifteen-year-old Thomasin, adolescent Caleb and the seven-year-old twins Mercy and Jonas stare wide-eyed as they are sentenced. To be excommunicated from the settlement was in essence a death sentence for the family.

Each character is richly written. The dynamics of each character and their interactions with one another are the basis of this story. William is a devout–albeit fanatical– man. His life is ruled by his interpretation of his faith. While he believes himself to be a righteous man and deserving of blessings bestowed by his God, his fellow Puritans perceive him to be

very self righteous. On the other hand, each member of his family perceives him in varying aspects which are told throughout the story. William's faith indicates that because he feels he is so righteous, his God will view him with favor and guide him in providing for and protecting his family. Throughout the film, as things begin to go wrong for the family William finds himself embroiled in a vicious cycle with his God. He prays and pleads with God to find favor with him and persecutes himself all the more because he feels the family's troubles are manifesting because he is not being devout enough or righteous enough.

Katherine is a fascinating character, and whereas William is ruled by his faith in God, Katherine is ruled by her fears. Her family's survival is the pinnacle of her fear. Katherine should be considered a good Puritan woman. However, her devotion to the Puritan God is almost non-existent–in fact, she barely mentions God throughout the film. Her adherence to the Puritan faith is completely indicated by going through the motions with William as the lead. Subsequently, when things go wrong for the family, Katherine's earthly explanation is placing the blame on William for failing the family and eventually she blames Thomasin as well. Katherine's faith that there is a Devil manifests in her belief that the Devil is working through Thomasin.

REBECCA HALLADAY

To read the rest of this feature article, please visit TheWitchesAlmanac.com/ pages/almanac-extras.

WITCHBLOOD:

The Book of Enoch and the Occult

An Excerpt From Harold Roth's
The Forbidden Knowledge of the Book of Enoch: The Watchers, Nephilim, Fallen Angels and the End of the World

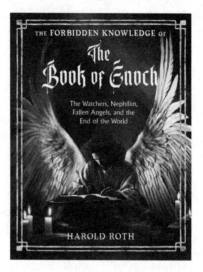

And Enoch walked with God,

and he was no longer,

for God had taken him.

–Genesis 5:24

MORE THAN two thousand years after it was written, *The Book of Enoch* continues to attract readers. Part of its attraction is the very fact that in almost no religious practice was it ever absorbed into the company of approved sacred texts. This gives the impression that Enoch was suppressed by the religious powers. On the contrary, it wasn't forbidden by any religion but simply lost its ability to represent the religion's doctrines as they changed.

It all starts with a kernel of a story mentioned in *Genesis* 6:1-8. Several generations after the creation of the first human beings, people already fill the Earth. A group of angels, the Watchers, look down and see how beautiful the daughters of human beings are. They go down to Earth and take human women for their wives. The Nephilim, murderous giants who are the children of the Watchers and their human wives, are the result, and a plague of violence explodes on Earth. The Nephilim have rapacious appetites of all kinds. They not only ate human beings, but each other, and they raped animals of all kinds. They killed most human beings on Earth before the Divine sent a flood to wipe them out. Only Noah, his family, and the animals on his arc were spared.

This story is greatly expanded in the oldest part of *Enoch*, *The Book of the Watchers*, which dates back to at least 300 BCE in Judea. But scholars believe that the stories it is based on go back even farther. Over and over, in all sorts of different cultures, we hear stories about heavenly beings coming down to Earth and interacting with human beings in some way, whether it be in the form of myths like Prometheus or Lucifer bringing fire or light to people, or modern tales of aliens inspiring and helping us. Clearly the concept of an interaction between Heaven and Earth has often been important to us.

At least two different, older tales were combined in *The Book of the Watchers*. One held the Watcher Shemihazah at its center, and the other the Watcher Asa'el. These two angels brought very different bodies of forbidden knowledge to human beings.

Shemihazah brought traditional occult arts like divination through all sorts of natural signs, from types of lightning to astrology; and dark arts like spellwork, including cursing and pacts. Asa'el brings the forbidden knowledge of metalwork, focusing on making armor, swords, and spears— the instruments of war, a way of distorting and debasing metalworking, changing it from forging instruments of agriculture, like hoes, shovels, and plows, to instruments of death. But like an old-time alchemist, he also brings the forbidden knowledge of dyes, silversmithing, and cosmetics. These are used by human beings, both men and women, to entice others into illicit sex, and that comes to be seen as the greater evil of the two bodies of forbidden knowledge the Watchers bring. *Enoch* sees Shemihazah and Asa'el as two completely different sources of evil.

Asa'el is mentioned in all sorts of items involved in Jewish magic. He's identified in spell books from the Cairo Genizah. His name is inscribed on Babylonian incantation bowls, written on amulets from the Land of Israel, and found in Greco-Egyptian magical texts like *The Greek Magical Papyri (PGM)*. In those works, he is not demonic or evil. On the contrary, he is an angel that magic workers can appeal to for help. To me, this says that he is possible to adjure in angel magic

William Blake's representation of Enoch

without the issue of raising a demon by accident. And for those who do work with demons, Asa'el is not a problem. Enoch himself is asked for help on some of the Babylonian incantation bowls. A few bowls mention Mount Hermon, which is where the Watchers made their oath to have sex with human women.

Some people believe in "witchblood"— an inherited, genetic feature peculiar to actual witches. Many of those who hold this idea believe that those born without witchblood cannot ever be witches. Some say this belief is modeled on the Enochic story of the Watchers coming down to Earth, having sex with women, and producing the Nephilim, who, in their belief, are the progenitors of this witchblood. But in my opinion, in no way could the Nephilim ever be the ancestors of witches, because for one thing, the Nephilim were completely unmagical. Remember, they raped and killed all human beings, they sexually assaulted and killed all the animals, including birds and fish, they killed and ate each other, and they despoiled the Earth. This does not sound like any sort of witchcraft to me. Not to mention that the Nephilim didn't have any children, which kind of negates any possibility that they were the ultimate source of witchblood.

The Watchers are another story. They brought forbidden knowledge to human beings, which included not only astrology but root-cutting, binding and reversing spells, and various methods of divination. These skills, not the brutality of the Nephilim, are treasures for magic workers. But remember with whom those skills were shared: people. If witches are to look back upon ancestors for inspiration, it should be not to the Nephilim or even the Watchers but to our human ancestors who received that knowledge and most likely maintained it. Also, for *Enoch*, magical knowledge is preserved in language, specifically, in writing. That makes a hash of the often-met objection that "real" magic is only passed on orally, especially when we recall how often a practice is interlaced with grimoire magic, for example, traditional (European) witchcraft, Vodou, and so forth. I think this kind of eclecticism is something to be proud of rather than to disdain. Being eclectic seems to be a fundamental human trait.

The story of angels coming to Earth and having children with women inspires modern practitioners of magic, especially when we consider the forbidden knowledge that the Watchers shared with humans. I understand that. But the Watchers story is not the only example of this in human culture.

In his introduction to *The Book of Enoch* the Prophet, magic practitioner Lon Milo DuQuette states that we don't know enough about *Enoch* to understand it. I think that this is true

If witches are to look back upon ancestors for inspiration, it should be not to the Nephilim or even the Watchers but to our human ancestors who received that knowledge and most likely maintained it.

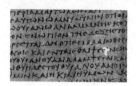

John Dee searched for Enoch for many years, perhaps because Enoch had a reputation as an astrologer and Dee was an astrologer himself.

for most of us, and it throws into relief the flaw in modeling ourselves after figures in the story. He also points out that the *Book of Enoch* that has come down to us doesn't have anything to do with Enochian magic, the Elizabethan astrologer and magician John Dee, the sorcerer Aleister Crowley, or any other prominent magician. He does mention Madame Blavatsky's book *The Secret Doctrine*, wherein she is quite fanciful about Enoch and who the Watchers represent. Personally, I cannot give her interpretation of the Watchers as alien spacemen any credibility. For me, alien spacemen have no place in magic or religion. They are a materialist incursion into the spiritual and magical universe, which can exist just fine without spacemen. Your lightyears may vary.

John Dee searched for *Enoch* for many years, perhaps because Enoch had a reputation as an astrologer and Dee was an astrologer himself. DuQuette wonders if perhaps Dee did have access to *Enoch* due to the

dispersion of the libraries of English abbeys from 1536-1539, but we don't find any note of it in his library catalogs or his own writings. He asked the angel Il about *Enoch* in 1583, and people often refer to his book about communing with angels as "Enoch."

Contrary to popular belief, Dee never referred to the angelic language as "Enochian." The angels told him it was called *Logaeth*. For me, the strongest connection between *Enoch* and Enochian magic is that both involved speaking with angels. But then so do the Picatrix, Hekhalot, and many other magical practices of various cultures.

Some have considered that Sloane MS. 3189, which contains the *Liber Logaeth (Book of the Speech of God)*, is the *Enoch*-related book that Dee refers to during his travels in 1586, but if you look at it, you can see it has nothing to do with *The Book of Enoch*. It is simply Dee's notes on his conversations with angels. You can see this and many other manuscripts at the

British Library's website, where they give access to a large and digitized collection of various things that help a person fiddle away hours of enjoyment.

One scholar's explanation for Dee's strong interest in finding *Enoch* ties that interest to the fear of a coming apocalypse and need to recover secret or lost knowledge to deal with such an event. This strikes me as pertinent to our own period—the scent of doom in the air has people scrambling for keys to understand and perhaps influence what is or will be occurring. I think this goes a long way toward explaining the intense interest in *Enoch* today.

—HAROLD ROTH

The Forbidden Knowledge of the Book of Enoch: The Watchers, Nephilim, Fallen Angels and the End of the World is available at redwheelweiser.com

Harold Roth is an author and artist and among the foremost authorities on plants within the modern occult community. He has studied Hebrew, as well as Jewish mysticism and magic for decades. The author of The Magic of the Sword of Moses and The Witching Herbs, Harold teaches classes on botanical magic, Kabbalah, and witchcraft. Visit him at haroldroth.com

The story of angels coming to Earth and having children with women inspires modern practitioners of magic, especially when we consider the forbidden knowledge that the Watchers shared with humans.

MOON GARDENING

BY PHASE

Sow, transplant, bud and graft   *Plow, cultivate, weed and reap*

NEW	First Quarter	FULL	Last Quarter	NEW
Plant above-ground crops with outside seeds, flowering annuals.	Plant above-ground crops with inside seeds.	Plant root crops, bulbs, biennials, perennials.		Do not plant.

BY PLACE IN THE ZODIAC

In general—plant and transplant crops that bear above ground when the Moon is in a watery sign: Cancer, Scorpio or Pisces. Plant and transplant root crops when the Moon is in Taurus or Capricorn; the other earthy sign, Virgo, encourages rot. The airy signs, Gemini, Libra and Aquarius, are good for some crops and not for others. The fiery signs, Aries, Leo and Sagittarius, are barren signs for most crops and best used for weeding, pest control and cultivating the soil.

♈

Aries—*barren, hot and dry.* Favorable for planting and transplanting beets, onions and garlic, but unfavorable for all other crops. Good for weeding and pest control, for canning and preserving, and for all activities involving fire.

♉

Taurus—*fruitful, cold and dry.* Fertile, best for planting root crops and also very favorable for all transplanting as it encourages root growth. Good for planting crops that bear above ground and for canning and preserving. Prune in this sign to encourage root growth.

♊

Gemini—*barren, hot and moist.* The best sign for planting beans, which will bear more heavily. Unfavorable for other crops. Good for harvesting and for gathering herbs.

♋

Cancer—*fruitful, cold and moist.* Best for planting crops that bear above ground and very favorable for root crops. Dig garden beds when the Moon is in this sign, and everything planted in them will flourish. Prune in this sign to encourage growth.

♌

Leo—*barren, hot and dry.* Nothing should be planted or transplanted while the Moon is in the Lion. Favorable for weeding and pest control, for tilling and cultivating the soil, and for canning and preserving.

♍

Virgo—*barren, cold and dry.* Good for planting grasses and grains, but unfavorable for other crops. Unfavorable for canning and preserving, but favorable for

46

weeding, pest control, tilling and cultivating. Make compost when the Moon is in the Virgin and it will ripen faster.

♎︎

Libra—*fruitful, hot and moist.* The best sign to plant flowers and vines and somewhat favorable for crops that bear above the ground. Prune in this sign to encourage flowering.

♏︎

Scorpio—*fruitful, cold and moist.* Very favorable to plant and transplant crops that bear above ground, and favorable for planting and transplanting root crops. Set out fruit trees when the Moon is in this sign and prune to encourage growth.

♐︎

Sagittarius—*barren, hot and dry.* Favorable for planting onions, garlic and cucumbers, but unfavorable for all other crops, and especially unfavorable for transplanting. Favorable for canning and preserving, for tilling and cultivating the soil, and for pruning to discourage growth.

♑︎

Capricorn—*fruitful, cold and dry.* Very favorable for planting and transplanting root crops, favorable for flowers, vines, and all crops that bear above ground. Plant trees, bushes and vines in this sign. Prune trees and vines to strengthen the branches.

♒︎

Aquarius—*barren, hot and moist.* Favorable for weeding and pest control, tilling and cultivating the soil, harvesting crops, and gathering herbs. Somewhat favorable for planting crops that bear above ground, but only in dry weather or the seeds will tend to rot.

♓︎

Pisces—*fruitful, cold and moist.* Very favorable for planting and transplanting crops that bear above ground and favorable for flowers and all root crops except potatoes. Prune when the Moon is in the Fishes to encourage growth. Plant trees, bushes and vines in this sign.

Consult our Moon Calendar pages for phase and place in the zodiac circle. The Moon remains in a sign for about two and a half days. Match your gardening activity to the day that follows the Moon's entry into that zodiacal sign. For best results, choose days when the phase and sign are both favorable. For example, plant seeds when the Moon is waxing in a suitable fruitful sign, and uproot stubborn weeds when the Moon is in the fourth quarter in a barren sign.

The MOON Calendar

is divided into zodiac signs rather than the more familiar Gregorian calendar.

2025

2026

Bear in mind that new projects should be initiated when the Moon is waxing (from dark to full). When the Moon is on the wane (from full to dark), it is a time for storing energy and the wise person waits.

Please note that Moons are listed by day of entry into each sign. Quarters are marked, but as rising and setting times vary from one region to another, it is advisable to check your local newspaper, library or planetarium.
The Moon's Place is computed for Eastern Time.

aries

March 20 – April 19, 2025
Cardinal Sign of Fire △ Ruled by Mars ♂

S	M	T	W	T	F	S
Pentagram—*Protection, balance, mysticism* The pentagram has a rich history dating back to ancient civilizations. In early Mesopotamia, it symbolized the five known planets and imperial power. Pythagoreans in ancient Greece revered this symbol as a sign of mathematical perfection and balance. During the Middle Ages, it became associated ⬇				Mar **20** Vernal Equinox Sagittarius	**21**	**22** Capricorn
23	**24** Aquarius	**25** *Beware of new competition*	**26**	**27** *Tarot's Hanged Man* Pisces	**28** Partial Solar eclipse ⇨	**29** Aries
30 WAXING *Recognize Mars*	**31** Taurus	April **1** All Fools Day	**2** *Roll the dice* Gemini	**3**	**4** Cancer	**5** *Cast a deep spell*
6 Leo	**7**	**8** *Be Silent* Virgo	**9**	**10** Libra	**11** *Shed a tear*	**12** Seed Moon
13 WANING Scorpio	**14** *Speak to Hecate*	**15** Sagittarius	**16** *Conjure a spirit*	**17**	**18** *Time to dance* Capricorn	

with Christian mysticism, representing the five wounds of Christ. In modern Neo-Pagan and Wiccan traditions, it embodies the unity of Earth, Air, Fire, Water and Spirit. Today the pentagram continues as a revered emblem in spiritual practices, symbolizing protection, balance and interconnectedness. In meditation, it is used to foster a sense of harmony and protection, grounding practitioners in the Elements and their inner strength. Moreover, the pentagram often features in rituals and ceremonies, serving as a powerful focal point for invoking spiritual energy.

The Oxen & the Wheels

A PAIR OF OXEN were drawing a heavily loaded wagon along a miry country road. They had to use all their strength to pull the wagon, but they did not complain.

The Wheels of the wagon were of a different sort. Though the task they had to do was very light compared with that of the Oxen, they creaked and groaned at every turn. The poor Oxen, pulling with all their might to draw the wagon through the deep mud, had their ears filled with the loud complaining of the Wheels. And this, you may well know, made their work so much the harder to endure.

"Silence!" the Oxen cried at last, out of patience. "What have you Wheels to complain about so loudly? We are drawing all the weight, not you, and we are keeping still about it besides."

They complain most who suffer least.

taurus
April 20 – May 20, 2025
Fixed Sign of Earth ♄ Ruled by Venus ♀

S	M	T	W	T	F	S
April **20** (Aquarius)	**21**	**22**	**23** Pisces	**24** Plant beans	**25** Sing to the stars Aries	**26**
27 Taurus	**28** WAXING	**29** Gemini	**30** Walpurgis Night	May **1** Beltane Cancer	**2** Gather dew	**3** Light fires Leo
4	**5** Carve a rune Virgo	**6**	**7** Learn a new spell	**8** White Lotus Day Libra	**9**	**10** Meditate with passion Scorpio
11 Vesak Day ⇨	**12** Hare Moon	**13** WANING Sagittarius	**14** Photograph flowers	**15** Capricorn	**16** Start a new job	**17**
18 Time to study Aquarius	**19**	**20** Pisces				

Ankh—*Immortality, life, protection* Known as the "key of life," this ancient Egyptian symbol has long been linked with life and immortality. Prominently featured in Egyptian art and hieroglyphs, it often appeared in the hands of deities, signifying their power to bestow life. It symbolized eternal life and the connection between the earthly and divine realms. Today, the ankh is embraced by various spiritual and cultural movements, including Neo-Paganism and Kemetic traditions. It is also used in magical traditions as a talisman for protection and healing rituals. In meditation, the ankh helps to connect with the life force, fostering a sense of continuity and spiritual insight. Additionally, the ankh is often worn as jewelry, not only for its aesthetic appeal but also for its spiritual significance, offering a constant reminder of life's sacred and enduring nature.

Notable Quotations

AIR

Every breath we take is a reminder that we are intimately connected to the cosmos, for the air is the very medium through which the universe expresses its divine essence.

Rumi

The air is the breath of the cosmos, carrying the whispers of eternity and the echoes of creation.

Hermann Hesse

What is brought by the wind, will be carried away by the wind.

Persian Proverb

For the breath of life is in the sunlight and the hand of life is in the wind.

Khalil Gibran

As we breathe in the air, we take in the very essence of existence, connecting with the cosmic rhythms that govern all life.

Ralph Waldo Emerson

The air is the only place free from prejudice.

Bessie Coleman

Now I see the secret of making the best person: it is to grow in the open air and to eat and sleep with the earth.

Walt Whitman

He lives most life whoever breathes most air.

Elizabeth Barrett Browning

In every breath, we inhale the essence of the universe, for the air is the breath of the cosmos itself.

Lao Tzu

The air we breathe is the exhalation of the universe, carrying within it the energy and vitality of all creation.

Paramahansa Yogananda

the invisible gift:
our purest, sweet necessity: the air.

Mary Oliver, Thirst

Quotes compiled by Isabel Kunkle.

gemini

May 21 – June 20, 2025

Mutable Sign of Air ♎ Ruled by Mercury ☿

S	M	T	W	T	F	S
Yin Yang—*Balance, harmony, unity* The concepts of duality and interdependence in the universe are beautifully captured by the yin yang symbol. Originating from Taoism, it embodies the concept that everything contains both yin (the dark, ↓			May **21**	**22** *Go first!* Aries	**23**	**24** *Work the garden* Taurus
25 *Express gratitude*	**26** ● Gemini	**27** WAXING	**28** *Be nostalgic* Cancer	**29** Oak Apple Day	**30** Leo	**31**
June **1** *Show joy*	**2** ◐ Virgo	**3**	**4** *Bond with a friend* Libra	**5** Night of the Watchers	**6** *Be serious* Scorpio	**7**
8 *Always say thank you*	**9** Sagittarius	**10** *Plan a trip*	**11** ◯ Dyad Moon	**12** WANING Capricorn	**13**	**14** *Play games* Aquarius
15	**16** *Ponder Family* Pisces	**17**	**18** ◑ Aries	**19** *Smile!*	**20** Summer Solstice Taurus	

passive, receptive) and yang (the light, active, creative) elements, which are in constant flux and balance. It is integrated into various aspects of Chinese culture, including medicine, martial arts and feng shui. The yin yang symbol remains a powerful emblem of balance and unity, transcending cultural boundaries to be embraced globally in various spiritual and philosophical contexts. It is often used in modern practices like yoga and meditation to promote inner peace and equilibrium. The enduring significance of the yin yang highlights its message of harmonious balance of life's dualities.

⋛ Willow ⋚

Saille

WILLOWS ARE magical trees with slender pale silver-green leaves. The weeping willow originated in China, where it graced cemeteries as a symbol of immortality, and the tree had spread to the Near East by Biblical times. An Old Testament reference to the exiled Jews hanging their harps upon the willows as they wept beside the rivers of Babylon led to the weeping willow's classification by Linnaeus as *Silax babylonica.* In ancient Greece, the Goddess Hera was born under a willow on the island of Samos, where a magnificent temple was built to honor her. In the underworld kingdom of Pluto and Persephone, Orpheus touched a willow branch and received the gift of supernatural eloquence. Willow groves are sacred to Hecate, dark Goddess of Witchcraft.

An old spell uses willow to dismiss love and transform passion into friendship. At Full Moon snip a foot-long tendril from a weeping willow tree and braid it with equal lengths of bright red and cool green yarn. Tie three knots in the braid and hang the charm in an airy room until the Moon is in its last quarter. On three successive nights untie the knots one by one in privacy and silence while concentrating on your desire. Before the New Moon rises, burn the red strand to ashes and throw to the winds. Coil the willow and green wool together and place in an envelope for safe-keeping.

The pussy willow is used in love charms as a guard against evil and its wands are often employed in divination. Reflecting the ancient status of the pussy willow, it is the wood to "knock on" and avert bad luck.

Medieval herbalists placed all willows under the rulership of the Moon.

—ELIZABETH PEPPER

54

cancer
June 21 – July 22, 2025
Cardinal Sign of Water ▽ *Ruled by Moon* ☽

CANCER

S	M	T	W	T	F	S
	All Seeing Eye—*Providence, protection, vision* This symbol of divine providence and omniscience is deeply embedded in mysticism and spirituality. Tracing its origins to ancient Egypt, it was known as the Eye of Horus, symbolizing protection, royal power and good health. It has appeared in various cultures and religions, often signifying an omnipresent, watchful force. In Freemasonry, the all-seeing eye denotes the watchful eye of ↓					June **21**
22 *Watch Sunrise* Gemini	**23** *Gather St. John's Wort*	**24** Midsummer Cancer	**25** ●	**26** WAXING	**27** *Remember a dream*	**28**
29 Virgo	**30** *Talk to a cat*	July **1** Libra	**2** ◑	**3** *Wear a favorite color*	**4** Scorpio	**5**
6 Sagittarius	**7** *Break a rule*	**8**	**9** Capricorn	**10** ○ Mead Moon	**11** WANING Aquarius	**12** *Sink into yourself*
13 Pisces	**14** *Draw with color*	**15**	**16** *Take a chance* Aries	**17** ◐	**18** *Call your best friend* Taurus	
20 Gemini	**21** *Attempt automatic writing*	**22** Cancer	the Great Architect of the Universe. It retains its mystical significance, frequently appearing in esoteric contexts to evoke higher consciousness. The all-seeing eye is often associated with secret societies and hidden knowledge. Its enduring presence across different cultures underscores its role as a symbol of wisdom and spiritual aspiration.			

Making A Wish Come True

The granting of a cherished wish has long been a popular pursuit among those who would practice the old ways. One technique which works very well dates from the Witcheries of ancient Rome and Greece. It involves a wish made by the beautiful nymph Daphne, the daughter of the river God Peneus. She spurned all of the eligible and handsome suitors who wooed her, much to the chagrin of her father—Peneus longed for a grandson. She begged her father to allow her to remain independent like Diana until he granted her the freedom to run joyfully into the deep forest. One day Apollo spotted her and was enchanted by Daphne's unique beauty. The sight of her, with her long hair wild and tangled and dressed in a knee length, short-sleeved tunic, made Apollo's heart blaze with the fire of love. He started off in pursuit. Daphne fled. Because she was a very fast runner, even Apollo found it a challenge to catch up. He begged her to stop and find out who he was, proclaiming his love for her. This terrified the free-spirited nymph more than ever and she realized that the situation was hopeless. She called out a wish to escape. The trees parted, revealing her father's river. Daphne's feet became roots and her skin turned to bark. The forest and water spirits turned her into a tree—she became the beautiful bay laurel. Apollo was grief stricken and claimed her as his own tree with branches to be used to make wreaths to crown his victors. Ever since, fragrant bay laurel leaves have been treasured. There is a tradition that the bay leaf will grant a heartfelt desire, a wish, for those who wish with the fervor of Daphne.

The Bay Leaf Wish Ritual
Select a large, whole bay leaf. Holding it carefully, speak your wish aloud. Then it can be written directly on the leaf or penned on a slip of paper which is wrapped around the leaf. Keep the leaf among your sacred objects, perhaps on your altar or in your journal. Within three days of a Full Moon the leaf can be burned and the ashes cast into either running water or the wind. Be sure to wish thoughtfully and carefully, because your request will probably be granted.

—GRANIA LING

leo

July 23 – August 22, 2025
Fixed Sign of Fire △ Ruled by Sun ☉

LEO

S	M	T	W	T	F	S
Ouroboros—**Eternity, renewal, transformation** A timeless symbol of a serpent or dragon consuming its own tail, the Ouroboros signifies the cyclical nature of life, death and rebirth. With origins in Egypt and Greece, it has long been an ↓			July **23** Ancient Egyptian New Year	**24** ● Leo	**25** WAXING	**26** *Look closely* Virgo
27	**28**	**29** Libra	**30** *Indulge in baking*	**31** Lughnassad Eve Scorpio	Aug **1** ◐	**2** Lammas ⇐
3 Sagittarius	**4**	**5** *Harvest Corn* Capricorn	**6**	**7**	**8** *Pray to Selene* Aquarius	**9** Wort Moon
10 WANING Pisces	**11** *Change a color*	**12** Aries	**13** Diana's Day	**14** Taurus	**15** *Show love*	**16** ◐ Gemini
17 Black Cat Appreciation Day	**18** *Gaze into a crystal* Cancer	**19**	**20** Leo	**21** *Water your plants*	**22**	

emblem of eternity. The Ouroboros encapsulates the endless cycle of destruction and creation, a concept central to alchemy. It maintains its mystical importance, frequently appearing in esoteric and spiritual contexts to symbolize the unity of the universe and the continuous renewal of life. The Ouroboros is also significant in psychological and philosophical discussions, where it represents introspection, wholeness and self-sufficiency. Its lasting presence in various cultures and epochs highlights its profound message of perpetual continuity and renewal, underscoring the interwoven nature of existence and the eternal cycle of life.

TAROT'S THE JUGGLER

THE JUGGLER

SINCE THE BEGINNING of recorded history, the skillful juggler has entertained his audience with his principal trick, which is depicted in this Tarot trump. The "Cups and Ball" trick uses three inverted Cups and a ball to misdirect his victims. The ball is seemingly placed under one cup, which is then switched around rapidly with the others. The unwary onlooker is now encouraged to bet money on which cup the ball is under. The design of our card is based upon another fifteenth century illustration of *The Children of the Planets*. The Juggler is at his table up to his old trick, baiting and switching, bamboozling gullible onlookers. Mercury, the astrological ruler of tricksters and wheeler-dealers, is the planet whose occult influence the Juggler falls under, as does the Juggler's pet monkey. Today we might see the Juggler as an entrepreneur, agent, sly lawyer or politician, fake psychic or swindler, depending on his position and the cards that surround him. His appearance in your spread implies the application of some form of skill, cunning, dexterity or diplomacy. Or maybe the enquirer is being conned and taken for a ride, depending on how the card is positioned, upright or reversed. NB—The Dame Fortune Tarot uses the Etteilla Tarot system for trumps and minor arcana.

Excerpted from Dame Fortune's Wheel Tarot—A Pictorial Key *by Paul Huson, published by The Witches' Almanac.*

virgo

August 23 – September 22, 2025

Mutable Sign of Earth ♍ Ruled by Mercury ☿

S	M	T	W	T	F	S
Triskelion—*Life, death and rebirth* With its three interlocking spirals, the Triskelion is a powerful symbol of motion, progress and cycles. Originating from ancient Celtic culture, it is often found on artifacts such as stones, jewelry and pottery, symbolizing the triadic nature of existence—life, death and rebirth. This ancient emblem also represented the three realms of material existence and spiritual growth. In modern times, the Triskelion ↓						Aug **23** Virgo
24 WAXING	**25** Libra	**26** Clean your altar	**27** Ganesha Chaturthi Scorpio	**28**	**29**	**30** Trees are our friends Sagittarius
31	Sep **1** Open a door Capricorn	**2**	**3**	**4** Consider your chart Aquarius	**5**	**6** Remember a past life Pisces
7 Barley Moon	**8** Total Lunar Eclipse ⇐ Aries	**9** WANING	**10** Share a meal Taurus	**11**	**12** Seize an opportunity Gemini	**13**
14 Cancer	**15**	**16** Light a candle	**17** Leo	**18**	**19** Change your mind Virgo	**20** Partial Solar Eclipse ⇨
21	**22** Autumnal Equinox Libra	is embraced by Neo-Pagan traditions, where it continues to symbolize spiritual growth, personal development and the cycles of life. The symbol is frequently adopted in meditation practices of pagan rituals to invoke dynamic energy and transformation. The lasting prominence of the Triskelion in art and spirituality underscores its profound connection to nature and its cycles. Its message of unity and perpetual motion resonates across many cultures.				

The Geomantic Figures: Puella

GEOMANCY IS AN ANCIENT SYSTEM of divination that uses sixteen symbols, the geomantic figures. Easy to learn and use, it was one of the most popular divination methods in the Middle Ages and Renaissance. It remained in use among rural cunning folk for many centuries thereafter, and is now undergoing a renaissance of its own as diviners discover its possibilities.

The geomantic figures are made up of single and double dots. Each figure has a name and a divinatory meaning, and the figures are also assigned to the four elements, the twelve signs of the Zodiac, the seven planets and the nodes of the Moon. The dots that make up the figures signify their inner meanings: the four lines of dots represent Fire, Air, Water and Earth, and show that the Elements are present in either active (one dot) or latent (two dots) form.

The seventh of the geomantic figures is Puella, which means Girl. Puella belongs to the element of Air, the Zodiacal sign Libra, and the planet Venus. The pattern of dots that forms this figure resembles a set of old-fashioned scales, with the two side dots as its pans, and also a human figure with breasts.

Read as symbols of the elements, the dots that form Puella reveal much about the nature of this figure. In this figure the elements of Fire, Water` and Earth are active, while Air is latent. It may seem surprising that Air, the one latent element, is also the element most closely associated with it, but subtle relationships of that kind are common in geomancy: as a figure of desire, Puella is defined by what it lacks.

In divination Puella stands for harmony and happiness that may not last indefinitely; it is a positive figure, but fickle. It is favorable for all questions involving love and relationships, and also for creative activities of all kinds and for luck. It is unfavorable in any question where stability is desired.

—JOHN MICHAEL GREER

libra

September 23 – October 22, 2025

Cardinal Sign of Air ♎ Ruled by Venus ♀

LIBRA

S	M	T	W	T	F	S
		Sep 23	24	· 25 Have patience Scorpio	26 Sagittarius	27
28	29 ◐ Capricorn	· 30	Oct 1 Perform a ritual Aquarius	2	3 Analyze a dream Pisces	4
5 Aries	6 ◯ Blood Moon	7 WANING Taurus	8 Charge your tools	9 Gemini	10 Effort brings change	11
12 Cancer	13 ◑	14 Pick your battles Leo	15	16 Protect your familiar Virgo	17	18
19 Libra	20 Honor the Dark Goddess	21 ●	22 WAXING Scorpio			

Hexagram—*Union, hope, transformation* Widely recognized as the Star of David, the Hexagram is a six-pointed star symbol that carries profound spiritual significance. Its origins are found in various ancient cultures, where it was used as a symbol of unity, balance and the interplay of opposites. In alchemy, the hexagram represents the harmony between male and female energies and the Elements of Fire and Water. Historically, it has been a symbol of protection and divine connection, appearing in talismans and magical rituals. Today the Star of David is not only a symbol of Judaism but is also utilized in diverse spiritual practices around the world, symbolizing balance, unity and the integration of the material and spiritual realms. Its persistent presence in various contexts underscores its enduring importance and multifaceted meanings.

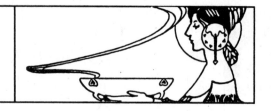

Soul Cakes

ON SAMHAIN, we take time to remember our ancestors and all those who have passed in the the last year. It is the time of the final harvest, the culling of domestic herds.

In Northern Europe the association of this time of the year with death and a fallow season is an ancient one that carried through the Middle Ages and into modern times.

Soul Cakes are small, round, spiced cakes, made for All Hallows' Eve (known as All Hallows or Samhain to some) to celebrate and commemorate the dead. The poor that went door to door *souling* or begging for alms were usually given a soul cake along with alms. Soul cakes were also given to mummers who made their rounds entertaining on All Hallows' Eve.

Traditional British song

Soul, Soul, a soul cake!
I pray thee, good missus, a soul cake!
One for Peter, two for Paul, three
  for Him what made us all!
Soul Cake, soul cake, please good
  missus, a soul cake!
An apple, a pear, a plum, or a cherry,
  any good thing to make us all merry.
One for Peter, two for Paul, &
  three for Him who made us all!

Making Soul Cakes

6 oz butter, softened
¾ cup caster sugar
3 egg yolks from large eggs
3 cups plain flour
2 tsp mixed spice
1 tsp allspice
2 tbsp milk
½ cup raisins or currants

Preheat the oven to 350°F.

Cream together the butter and sugar until pale yellow and fluffy. Doing this by hand is best and is a good time to chant out the names of your beloved dead. When the butter-sugar mix is creamy in consistency, beat in the egg yolks. Stir in the flour, mixed spice, allspice and the raisins (or currants.) Mix in the milk one tablespoon at a time, so as not to add too much. Just enough milk should be added so that the dough can be brought together by hand without being sticky to touch.

Roll out the dough on a floured surface to the thickness ¼", using a 2" cookie cutter to stamp out the cakes. Place the cakes on a baking sheet lined with baking paper. Finally, use a knife to mark an equilateral cross on each cake. Bake in the oven for 13–15 minutes. They will be done when they are lightly golden.

–DEVON STRONG

scorpio

October 23 – November 21, 2025

Fixed Sign of Water ▽ Ruled by Pluto ♀

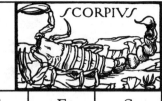

⟨CORPIVⱮ

S	M	T	W	T	F	S
Flower of Life—*Harmony, interconnection, unity* The intricate geometry of overlapping circles, known as the Flower of Life, has fascinated civilizations for centuries. Found in diverse cultures worldwide, it symbolizes the fundamental patterns of existence and the interconnectedness of all life. In sacred geometry, this design is seen as a ⬇				Oct **23**	**24** Sagittarius	**25**
26 *Write a friend* Capricorn	**27**	**28** *Close your eyes* Aquarius	**29** ◑	**30** *Honor the dead*	**31** Samhain Eve Pisces	Nov **1** Hallowmas
2 *Mighty protectors speak* Aries	**3**	**4** *Remember loved ones* Taurus	**5** ◯ Snow Moon	**6** WANING Gemini	**7**	**8** *Never forget* Cancer
9 *Lions roar*	**10** Leo	**11**	**12** ◐	**13** *Light incense* Virgo	**14**	**15** *Play a game* Libra
16 Hecate Night	**17** Scorpio	**18** *Plan a time of joy*	**19** ● Sagittarius	**20** WAXING	**21**	

blueprint for creation, illustrating the harmony and structure of the universe. Ancient Egyptians and Greeks integrated it into their art and architecture, attributing deep spiritual significance to its form. Today, the Flower of Life is embraced by various spiritual traditions and New Age practices, symbolizing unity, wholeness and cosmic order. It is commonly used in meditation and healing practices to promote a sense of balance, enlightenment and spiritual growth. The widespread use and reverence of the Flower of Life underscore its lasting impact and the profound insights it provides into the nature of reality and existence.

The Eyes of Buddha and Sacred Chant

The eyes of Buddha symbolize the duality of wisdom and compassion. Below these eyes is the mantra, "Om Mani Padme Hum," which expresses the idea of "Behold! The jewel in the lotus."

sagittarius

November 22 – December 21, 2025

Mutable Sign of Fire △ Ruled by Jupiter ♃

S	M	T	W	T	F	S
	Caduceus—*Integration, transformation, healing* Characterized by two serpents entwined around a staff, the Caduceus originates from Greek mythology and is associated with Hermes, the messenger God who guided souls to the afterlife. The Caduceus represents trade, negotiation and balance, reflecting Hermes' role as a mediator. In ancient times, it also symbolized alchemical processes and ↓					Nov **22** Capricorn
23	**24**	**25** *Be foolish!* Aquarius	**26**	**27** Pisces	**28** 🌓	**29** Aries
30	Dec **1** *Cleanse your home* Taurus	**2**	**3** *Change voices* Gemini	**4** 🌕 Oak Moon	**5** WANING Cancer	**6**
7 *Enjoy cool sunshine* Leo	**8**	**9** *Give someone space*	**10** Virgo	**11** 🌓	**12** *Spin the wheel* Libra	**13**
14 *First frost*	**15** *Leave an offering* Scorpio	**16** Fairy Queen Eve	**17** Saturnalia Sagittarius	**18** *Read the tarot*	**19** 🌑	**20** WAXING Capricorn
21 Winter Solstice	the transformative power of healing. Today the Caduceus is widely recognized in the medical field, though often confused with the Rod of Asclepius, the true symbol of medicine. Its use extends to various spiritual practices where it embodies the integration of dualities, such as life and death or health and illness. The Caduceus continues to be a powerful emblem, reflecting themes of harmony, balance and the dynamic interplay of opposites in both historical and modern contexts.					

Chinese Astrology
The Next Step

THE LUNAR Calendar, Oriental and Chinese Zodiac are all names used throughout the Far East—from China and Japan to Vietnam and Sri Lanka and Korea—to identify the 12 year calendar of animal zodiac signs followed by millions. The Lunar New Year begins on the second New Moon following the Winter Solstice. The calendar's composition is based on five elements, further distinguishing the traits of the animal signs. The final digit of the Gregorian calendar years used in the West will reveal which element guides the current animal's year.

Years ending in   0,1 are Metal
                         2,3 are Water
                         4,5 are Wood
                         6,7 are Fire
                         8, 9 are Earth

Key Words and visible planets are linked to each of the five Elements:

Metal, Venus, white, silver: prosperous, practical, strong, determined, opinionated

Water, Mercury, black, deep blue: communicates, emotional, intuitive, diplomatic

Wood, Jupiter, green: sociable, generous, leadership, kindness

Fire, Mars, red, pink, purple: confident, adventurous, assertive, innovative

Earth, Saturn, yellow, brown: trustworthy, stable, methodical, serious

—DIKKI-JO MULLEN

capricorn

December 21 2025 – January 19, 2026
Cardinal Sign of Earth ♀ Ruled by Saturn ♄

S	M	T	W	T	F	S
	Dec **22**	**23**	**24**	**25**	**26**	**27**
		Gather Holly		*Sing Yuletide carols*		
	Aquarius		Pisces			Aries
28	**29**	**30**	**31** Jan **1**		**2**	**3**
			Listen to music		*Use the black mirror*	*Wolf Moon*
Ring bells	Taurus		Gemini		Cancer	
4	**5**	**6**	**7**	**8**	**9**	**10**
WANING		*Gift a gemstone*		*Maintain respect*	*Feast of Janus*	
Leo		Virgo		Libra		
11	**12**	**13**	**14**	**15**	**16**	**17**
	Don't go too deep		*Sweep the house*	*Make a snowman*		
Scorpio		Sagittarius			Capricorn	
18	**19**					
	WAXING					
	Aquarius					

Dharmachakra—*Cycles, spirituality, progression* Representing the teachings of Buddha, the Dharmachakra, or Wheel of Dharma, is a profound symbol in Buddhism. It is traditionally depicted as a wheel with eight spokes, each representing the Noble Eightfold Path that guides practitioners toward enlightenment. The Dharmachakra's origins trace back to ancient India, where it was used in various religious and philosophical contexts to symbolize the cyclical nature of life and the universe. In Buddhist art and iconography, the wheel signifies the dissemination of Buddha's teachings and the ongoing cycle of birth, life, death and rebirth. Today it remains a central emblem in Buddhist practice and philosophy, symbolizing the pursuit of truth and spiritual progression. The Dharmachakra is also a powerful reminder of the interconnectedness of all things and the path to spiritual awakening, reflecting its enduring significance in both historical and contemporary spiritual contexts.

If you want to find the secrets of the universe, think in terms of energy, frequency and vibration.

—NIKOLA TESLA

aquarius

January 20 – February 18, 2026

Fixed Sign of Air ♎ Ruled by Uranus ♅

S	M	T	W	T	F	S
		Jan **20**	**21** *Wrap in a blanket* Pisces	**22**	**23** Aries	**24**
25 (moon) Taurus	**26**	**27** *Dream of two* Gemini	**28**	**29** Cancer	**30** *Play with pets*	**31** Oimelc Eve ⇨ Leo
Feb **1** (Storm Moon)	**2** WANING Candlemas Virgo	**3**	**4** *Share a vision*	**5** Libra	**6** *Talk to clouds*	**7** Scorpio
8	**9** (moon)	**10** *Cleanse your cards* Sagittarius	**11**	**12** *Drum for the spirits* Capricorn	**13**	**14** *Wear red*
15 Lupercalia Aquarius	**16** Chinese New Year ⇨ 	**17** (moon) Pisces	**18** Partial Solar Eclipse ⇦			

Sri Yantra—*Energy, harmony, order* A mesmerizing geometric design, the Sri Yantra, has been revered for centuries in Hindu tradition. Comprised of nine interlocking triangles that radiate from a central point, it symbolizes the cosmos and divine union of masculine and feminine energies. This ancient symbol is used in meditative practices and rituals, to channel spiritual energy and promote inner harmony. The Sri Yantra represents the abode of the deities and the path to spiritual enlightenment. In contemporary spirituality, it continues to be a powerful tool for meditation and manifestation, often used to focus the mind and attain higher states of consciousness. The Sri Yantra remains a potent emblem of spiritual growth, cosmic order and the pursuit of enlightenment.

THE ODD SLIPPER

WHILE TRAVELING in an Eastern country, Mr. Palomar bought a pair of slippers in a bazaar. Returning home, he tries to put them on. He realizes that one slipper is wider than the other and will not stay on his foot. He recalls the old vendor crouched on his heels in a niche of the bazaar in front of a pile of slippers of every size at random. He sees the man as he rummages in the pile to find a slipper suited to the customer's foot. He has him try it on and then starts rummaging again to hand him the presumed mate, which Mr. Palomar accepts without trying it on.

"Perhaps now," Mr. Palomar thinks, "another man is walking around that country with a mismatched pair of slippers." He sees a slender shadow moving over the desert with a limp, a slipper falling off his foot at every step or else, too tight, imprisoning a twisted foot. "Perhaps he, too, is thinking of me at this moment and hoping to run into me and make the trade. The relationship binding us is more concrete and clear than many of the relationships established between human beings. And yet we will never meet." He decides to go on wearing these odd slippers out of solidarity with his unknown companion in misfortune, to keep alive this complementary relationship that is so rare, this mirroring of limping steps from one continent to another.

—Italo Calvino, *Mr. Palomar*, translated from the Italian
by William Weaver (Harvest)

pisces

February 19 – March 20, 2026

Mutable Sign of Water ▽ *Ruled by Neptune* ♆

S	M	T	W	T	F	S
Labyrinth—*Journey, introspection, searching* With its winding paths and singular route, the labyrinth has long fascinated humanity, serving as a potent symbol of the spiritual journey. Unlike a maze, a labyrinth has one continuous path leading to the center and back out, representing introspection, pilgrimage and the journey toward ↓				Feb **19** *Turn around* Aries	**20** *Be blessed*	**21** Taurus
22	**23** *Consider the snow-flakes*	**24** 🌓 Gemini	**25**	**26** Cancer	**27** *Wolves howl*	**28** Leo
Mar **1** Matronalia	**2** *Count the trees* Virgo	**3** 🌑 Chaste Moon	**4** Total Lunar Eclipse ⇐ Libra	**5** WANING	**6** *Gaze into ice*	**7** Scorpio
8	**9** Sagittarius	**10** *Anger escalates*	**11** 🌓	**12** *Close the door* Capricorn	**13** *Carry copper*	**14** Aquarius
15 *Leprechaun Luck*	**16** Pisces	**17** *Break a curse*	**18** 🌑	**19** WAXING Minerva's Day Aries	**20**	

enlightenment Ancient Greeks and Egyptians incorporated labyrinths into their mythologies and sacred rituals, using them as metaphors for life's complexities and the search for deeper meaning. In medieval Europe, labyrinths were embedded in cathedral floors as aids for contemplative prayer and meditation. Today labyrinths are found in diverse spiritual contexts, from churches and retreat centers to public parks, where they serve as tools for meditation, stress reduction and personal reflection. Their enduring presence in various traditions highlights their universal appeal and the timeless quest for self-discovery and spiritual growth.

for Hermes

Hail He who travels swiftly with a message on his lips,
　　who slips through the shadows unnoticed,
　　　　who dances on the hillsides with joy.

master of commerce,
prince of thieves,
immortal shepherd,
guide of souls...
who can elude your charm
　　or resist your guile?

Equally at ease in the madness of the marketplace,
　　in the mountains and meadows of Arkadia,
　　　　or the palace of Hades.

You know no limits.
You cross all boundaries.
Hail Hermes,
God of the crossroads!

　　　　　　　　　　–Sparrow

A modern interpretation of Kokopelli

TRICKSTER GODS OF THE WORLD

TRICKSTER GODS are archetypal figures found in diverse mythologies, embodying a complex fusion of chaos and creativity, wisdom and folly. These mischievous entities defy societal norms, challenging established structures and questioning the status quo. Their unpredictable nature often manifests in cunning pranks, shape-shifting abilities and a penchant for challenging authority. Despite their seemingly capricious actions, trickster Gods play integral roles in the cosmologies they inhabit.

The essence of trickster Gods lies in their ability to traverse boundaries and blur dichotomies. They exist at crossroads both literal and symbolic—places where choices are made and fate is determined. As mediators between the divine and mortal realms, tricksters are catalysts for change, pushing individuals and societies to confront the unexpected and navigate the complexities of existence. In their disruptive antics, these Gods bring about transformation, challenging people to reassess their perspectives and adapt to the ever-changing nature of reality.

While they are often associated with chaos, trickster Gods also serve as agents of creation and renewal. By breaking down established norms, they pave the way for innovation and new possibilities. The trickster archetype is a reminder that life's journey is inherently unpredictable, requiring adaptability and a sense of humor. Despite the challenges they pose, trickster Gods are not malevolent entities—rather, they offer valuable lessons about the dynamic, interconnected nature of the universe and the need for balance between order and disorder in the grand tapestry of mythology and human experience.

Here are some examples of trickster Gods in various world mythologies:

Loki (Norse): A pivotal figure in Norse mythology, Loki is the cunning and shape-shifting God of mischief and chaos. A complex character, he is both a companion and adversary to the Aesir Gods. Loki's origins are enigmatic—he is born of giants but counted among the Aesir through blood oaths. Known for his wit, charisma and ability to change forms, Loki's pranks range from harmless to disastrous, causing strife and testing the Gods' resilience. His most notorious act was orchestrating the death of Balder, which led to his punishment and eventual role in Ragnarök, the apocalyptic end of the Norse cosmos—a fate in which Loki plays a crucial, ambiguous role.

Coyote (Native American): A revered figure in Native American mythology, Coyote embodies the essence of the trickster archetype across diverse North American Indigenous cultures. Often depicted as a cunning, shape-shifting character, Coyote is both creator and disruptor, representing the duality of wisdom and folly. In various Native American traditions, Coyote plays a central role in creation myths, teaching essential lessons through clever exploits.

A modern interpretation of Loki

As a mediator between the natural and supernatural realms, Coyote's unpredictable nature challenges societal norms, highlighting the complexity of human experience. His presence resonates with adaptability and resilience in the ever-changing facets of the natural world.

Anansi (African): Anansi, the legendary spider trickster from the folklore of the Akan people of West Africa, weaves intricate tales that transcend time and culture. Revered as a master storyteller and sly schemer, Anansi is a shape-shifting deity whose cunning exploits range from outsmarting other animals to acquiring the world's stories. With a knack for turning the tables on more powerful beings, Anansi symbolizes not only the cleverness inherent in survival but also the transformative power of storytelling. As a cultural icon, Anansi bridges generations, imparting wisdom, wit and the enduring legacy of oral traditions across the African diaspora.

Hermes and Mercury (Greek and Roman): the swift-footed messenger of the Greek Gods, Hermes and his Roman counterpart Mercury embody the archetype of the clever trickster as well as acting as guides between realms. Known for his agility, Hermes bridges the divine and mortal, facilitating both communication and commerce. As the patron of travelers, thieves and eloquence, he wields the *caduceus*, a staff entwined with serpents. The Roman Mercury mirrors Hermes' roles, emphasizing swiftness and multifaceted influence. Both Gods symbolize the fluidity of boundaries from language to trade, embodying the transcendent nature of communication and the interconnectedness of the spiritual and material worlds.

Dionysus (Greek): Dionysus, revelry and ecstasy, personifies the dual nature of joy and chaos. As the liberator from social norms, his presence invokes spontaneous celebration and uninhibited revelry. Born of Zeus and a mortal, Dionysus traverses both divine and human realms, representing the fluidity of boundaries. Often depicted with a *thyrsus*—a fennel staff crowned with ivy—he inspires divine madness and creative ecstasy. The Bacchic rites dedicated to him celebrated the transformative power of wine and theater, honoring the unpredictable and liberating forces that challenge societal structures and embracing the inherent wildness of existence.

Eshu (Yoruba): A prominent figure in Yoruba mythology, Eshu serves as the mischievous messenger and trickster deity, intricately linked with the concept of destiny. Operating at crossroads both physical and metaphorical, Eshu is the mediator between Gods and humans, delivering offerings and influencing the Fates. His playful, unpredictable nature brings both blessings and challenges, reflecting the Yoruba worldview's intricate balance of forces. Often portrayed with a walking stick and a hat tilted in different directions, Eshu embodies the multifaceted aspects of existence where choices and paths intersect, revealing the nuanced interplay of destiny and human agency.

Sun Wukong (Chinese): The Monkey King from Chinese mythology, Sun Wukong is a formidable trickster with unmatched strength and magical prowess. Born from a stone, he rebels against divine authority, challenging heaven itself. Armed with a magical staff capable of endless transformations, Sun Wukong jour-

Kneeling figure of Eshu

neys westward in the epic *Journey to the West*, in which he aids the monk Xuanzang. His irreverent nature, resilience and resourcefulness represent an indomitable spirit in the face of cosmic challenges. Despite his mischief, Sun Wukong's loyalty and enlightenment make him a revered figure embodying the triumph of perseverance, wisdom and the pursuit of spiritual growth.

Krishna (Hindu Mythology): A central deity in Hindu mythology, Krishna embodies divine playfulness, wisdom and profound love. As the eighth avatar of Lord Vishnu, he navigates the cosmic dance of creation and destruction. Often depicted as a charismatic, flute-playing cowherd, Krishna enchants devotees with his divine melodies. His exploits—especially in the epic *Mahabharata*—convey timeless lessons on duty, righteousness and devotion. The divine lover in the Radha-Krishna tradition, he symbolizes the soul's yearning for union with the divine. Krishna's multifaceted nature encompasses both the mischievous child who steals butter and the

A mandala for Krishna

transcendent philosopher imparting spiritual truths.

Hotei (Japanese Buddhism): Hotei, the Laughing Buddha in Japanese Buddhism, radiates joy and contentment. Often depicted as a portly, bald monk with a wide smile, Hotei is a symbol of happiness and abundance. Embracing simplicity, he carries a cloth sack of treasures, sharing good fortune and laughter with those he encounters. As a guardian of children and patron of bartenders and the poor, Hotei's infectious laughter embodies the Zen philosophy of finding joy in the present moment and cultivating a compassionate, carefree spirit. His presence inspires a sense of well-being, reminding believers of the profound beauty in life's simple pleasures.

Eleggua (Santería and Yoruba): Eleggua, a revered deity in Santería and Yoruba traditions, is the mischievous guardian of crossroads and opener of paths. Often depicted as a child or an old man, Eleggua holds a key role in the Orisha pantheon. As a trickster figure, he governs communication, fortune and the choices individuals make at life's intersections. Devotees seek his guidance and blessings, recognizing his pivotal role in mediating between the spiritual and earthly realms. Eleggua's unpredictable nature reflects the complexities of destiny, emphasizing the importance of balance and wise decision making on life's intricate journey.

Nasreddin Hodja (Middle Eastern): Nasreddin Hodja, a legendary figure in Middle Eastern folklore, is a witty and wise trickster whose humorous anecdotes convey profound truths. Dressed in a distinctive turban and riding a donkey, Hodja navigates the complexities of life through clever banter and comical situations. As a teacher and folk hero, his tales transcend borders, imparting timeless lessons with humor and insight. Whether outsmarting authority figures or offering unconventional wisdom, Nasreddin Hodja serves as a cultural touchstone, embodying the enduring power of laughter and cleverness in navigating the challenges of everyday existence.

Legba (Vodou): Legba is a revered deity in Vodou and related African diasporic religions. The intermediary between the divine and human realms, he is guardian of the crossroads and opener of the gates. Often depicted as an old man or a child, Legba's playful and mischievous nature belies his crucial role in facilitating communication and spiritual access. Devotees seek his guidance and offerings at crossroads, recognizing his ability to unlock opportunities and connect with other spirits. As the Opener of the Way, Legba is central to Vodou ceremonies, embodying the interplay of choice and destiny at the crossroads of life's intricate journey.

Manabozho (Ojibwe): A prominent trickster figure in Ojibwe mythology, Manabozho embodies both the foolish and wise aspects of humanity. Also known as Nanabozho, he is a shapeshifter who takes various forms to navigate the world and teach essential life lessons. Manabozho's adventures shape the Ojibwe cosmos and culture, blending humor with profound teachings.

The veve for the Voudoun spirit Legba

From creating landscapes to outsmarting rivals, his cunning exploits convey the dual nature of human experience—balancing wisdom and folly. Revered as a cultural hero, Manabozho's narratives emphasize resilience, adaptability and the significance of laughter in confronting the challenges of existence.

Kokopelli (Native American): A revered figure in various Native American cultures, Kokopelli is a flute-playing deity symbolizing fertility, joy and transformation. Often depicted as a humpbacked flute player with a whimsical demeanor, Kokopelli's music is believed to bring about the changing seasons and encourage fertility in crops and animals. As a trickster and storyteller, he embodies the fluidity of life's cycles and the interconnectedness of nature. Kokopelli's presence is a celebration of the creative forces that shape existence, encouraging joy and growth through the transformative power of music, dance and the perpetual cycle of life's rebirth.

—AMELIA INGRAM

Early Spring
Opens a door in Heaven
From skies of glass
A Jacob's Ladder falls
On greening grass,
And o'er the mountain wall
Young angels pass.

...

O, follow, leaping blood,
the season's lure!
O heart, look down and up,
serene, secure,
Warm as the crocus cup,
like snow-drops, pure.
—TENNYSON

DION FORTUNE'S SPRINGTIDE

THE ELEMENT of Air is traditionally associated with the season of Spring. Enter Violet Mary Firth—Dion Fortune—age 15. Two volumes of her childhood poetry were privately published by her parents, *Violets* in 1904 and *More Violets* in 1906. The books received quite favorable reviews in two UK newspapers on July 8, 1905 in *The Sphere* and on March 14, 1906 in *The Bystander.* Many of her childhood musings shared below were about Spring.

So much has been written about Spring in both prose and poetry that little remains to be said. Perhaps the reason that it has received so much attention is that it is the most beautiful of all seasons. The roses of Summer are lovely, but they do not excel the daffodil, which gilds the riverside meadows in early Spring; nor can the reds of Autumn compare with the pale green of a newly-opened bud.

Perhaps we appreciate Spring's loveliness so much because we have fasted while the countryside was covered with snow, and now we feast our eyes upon a transformation which appears the more lovely when contrasted with the previous season's quiescence; and by the time Summer appears, we have been surfeited by the sweets of her predecessor, and do not appreciate, as fully as we might otherwise have done, her richer beauties.

As soon as last year's leaves had fallen, small brown knobs were visible upon the twigs and branches of the trees; during the Winter these remained dormant, but as soon as the warmth of Spring quickened the chilled sap into renewed activity, they began to swell, and ere long burst the dull outer coat and exposed to view the delicate green leaves within.

A sudden transformation now takes place; the landscape no longer wears the sombre colours of Winter, it seems as if some magician's brush has passed over the land from south to north, painting all the country green. The trees have opened their leaf-buds, or shaken out their catkins, which cast on the wind clouds of yellow pollen that drift across the open meadow-land, fertilising all female flowers in their path.

Other trees do not trust their precious dust to the capricious breezes, but secrete the honey which tempts the small wild bees to brave the uncertain weathers of an English Spring, and at the same time perform an involuntary service for their hosts.

The insect life is also awake; in sunny hedgerows beetles are beginning to appear, and the ants are working furiously to repair and extend their subterranean homes.

The appearance of the insects only heralds the approach of the insectivores, and from over the seas ever increasing streams of bird visitors are arriving.

Our own bats, too, who have slept away the Winter, now reappear, and the brisk snap of their little jaws as they catch a fly can be heard quite plainly on a still evening.

The flowers are by no means the least beautiful part of this altogether lovely season. Spring is heralded in by the snowdrop and wild violet; the climax of its reign is reached when the daffodil and cowslip are in flower, and it is ushered out by the pink petals of the dog-rose.

That the human life has a Springtime as well as Nature, has been declared many times, but the mental life has one also; when the buds of child-thought begin to grow into the full leaf of the mature mind, we call it Expansion.

When the spiritual search for Truth results in the discovery of perfect peace and understanding, it is called Revelation.

Yet these three, the Natural, Mental, and Spiritual Springtides, are the same process working in different spheres of life, and might be classed together under the one name of The Awakening.

MORE VIOLETS

27TH MARCH, 1905

If you are familiar with the corpus of Dion Fortune's Work, it is glaringly apparent the lay-psychoanalyst and Magician she would become. The "seeds" were there from the very beginning!

—THEA

2025 SUNRISE AND SUNSET TIMES

Providence—San Francisco—Sydney—London

	Sunrise				Sunset			
	Prov	**SF**	**Syd**	**Lon**	**Prov**	**SF**	**Syd**	**Lon**
Jan 5	7:13 AM	7:26 AM	5:52 AM	8:05 AM	4:28 PM	5:04 PM	8:08 PM	4:06 PM
15	7:11 AM	7:24 AM	6:00 AM	7:59 AM	4:39 PM	5:14 PM	8:07 PM	4:20 PM
25	7:04 AM	7:19 AM	6:10 AM	7:49 AM	4:51 PM	5:25 PM	8:03 PM	4:37 PM
Feb 5	6:54 AM	7:10 AM	6:21 AM	7:32 AM	5:05 PM	5:37 PM	7:56 PM	4:56 PM
15	6:41 AM	6:59 AM	6:31 AM	7:14 AM	5:18 PM	5:48 PM	7:46 PM	5:15 PM
25	6:27 AM	6:46 AM	6:40 AM	6:54 AM	5:30 PM	5:58 PM	7:35 PM	5:33 PM
Mar 5	6:14 AM	6:35 AM	6:47 AM	6:37 AM	5:40 PM	6:06 PM	7:25 PM	5:47 PM
15	6:57 AM	7:21 AM	6:55 AM	6:15 AM	6:51 PM	7:16 PM	7:12 PM	6:04 PM
25	6:40 AM	7:05 AM	7:02 AM	5:52 AM	7:02 PM	7:25 PM	6:58 PM	6:21 PM
Apr 5	6:22 AM	6:49 AM	7:11 AM	6:27 AM	7:14 PM	7:35 PM	6:44 PM	7:39 PM
15	6:06 AM	6:35 AM	6:18 AM	6:05 AM	7:25 PM	7:44 PM	5:31 PM	7:56 PM
25	5:51 AM	6:21 AM	6:26 AM	5:44 AM	7:36 PM	7:53 PM	5:19 PM	8:13 PM
May 5	5:37 AM	6:10 AM	6:33 AM	5:26 AM	7:47 PM	8:03 PM	5:09 PM	8:29 PM
15	5:26 AM	6:00 AM	6:41 AM	5:09 AM	7:58 PM	8:11 PM	5:01 PM	8:44 PM
25	5:18 AM	5:53 AM	6:47 AM	4:56 AM	8:07 PM	8:20 PM	4:55 PM	8:58 PM
June 5	5:12 AM	5:49 AM	6:54 AM	4:47 AM	8:16 PM	8:27 PM	4:52 PM	9:11 PM
15	5:11 AM	5:48 AM	6:59 AM	4:44 AM	8:21 PM	8:32 PM	4:52 PM	9:18 PM
25	5:13 AM	5:50 AM	7:01 AM	4:45 AM	8:23 PM	8:34 PM	4:54 PM	9:20 PM
July 5	5:18 AM	5:54 AM	7:01 AM	4:52 AM	8:22 PM	8:33 PM	4:58 PM	9:17 PM
15	5:25 AM	6:01 AM	6:58 AM	5:02 AM	8:17 PM	8:29 PM	5:03 PM	9:09 PM
25	5:34 AM	6:08 AM	6:53 AM	5:15 AM	8:09 PM	8:23 PM	5:10 PM	8:57 PM
Aug 5	5:45 AM	6:18 AM	6:45 AM	5:31 AM	7:57 PM	8:12 PM	5:17 PM	8:40 PM
15	5:55 AM	6:26 AM	6:35 AM	5:47 AM	7:44 PM	8:00 PM	5:24 PM	8:21 PM
25	6:05 AM	6:35 AM	6:23 AM	6:03 AM	7:28 PM	7:47 PM	5:31 PM	8:00 PM
Sept 5	6:16 AM	6:44 AM	6:09 AM	6:20 AM	7:10 PM	7:31 PM	5:38 PM	7:36 PM
15	6:27 AM	6:52 AM	5:55 AM	6:36 AM	6:53 PM	7:15 PM	5:45 PM	7:13 PM
25	6:37 AM	7:01 AM	5:41 AM	6:52 AM	6:36 PM	7:00 PM	5:52 PM	6:50 PM
Oct 5	6:48 AM	7:10 AM	6:28 AM	7:08 AM	6:19 PM	6:45 PM	6:59 PM	6:27 PM
15	6:59 AM	7:19 AM	6:15 AM	7:25 AM	6:02 PM	6:30 PM	7:07 PM	6:05 PM
25	7:10 AM	7:29 AM	6:03 AM	7:42 AM	5:47 PM	6:17 PM	7:15 PM	5:45 PM
Nov 5	6:24 AM	6:40 AM	5:52 AM	7:02 AM	4:33 PM	5:05 PM	7:25 PM	4:25 PM
15	6:36 AM	6:51 AM	5:44 AM	7:19 AM	4:23 PM	4:57 PM	7:35 PM	4:10 PM
25	6:48 AM	7:01 AM	5:39 AM	7:35 AM	4:17 PM	4:51 PM	7:44 PM	3:58 PM
Dec 5	6:58 AM	7:11 AM	5:38 AM	7:50 AM	4:14 PM	4:49 PM	7:53 PM	3:52 PM
15	7:07 AM	7:18 AM	5:39 AM	8:00 AM	4:14 PM	4:51 PM	8:00 PM	3:50 PM
25	7:12 AM	7:24 AM	5:44 AM	8:06 AM	4:19 PM	4:55 PM	8:06 PM	3:55 PM

Prov=Providence; SF=San Francisco; Syd=Sydney; Lon=London
Times are presented in the standard time of the geographical location, using the current time zone of that place.

Window on the Weather

THE ROLE of the the Sun and other natural cyclical influences on human herd behaviors has become even more evident in recent decades, as abundant data from scientific sources becomes widespread. One example of the remarkable variability of the Sun's heat output and geomagnetic influences through eleven-year solar cycles is the heat distribution of Earth's oceans. The alternating patterns of vast warm and cool water pools across the Pacific Ocean are commonly known as ENSO events—El Niño Southern Oscillation. This term includes variances of well-covered El Niño and La Niña episodes. Typically, El Niño conditions are wetter and cooler and La Niña conditions are warmer and dryer. The resulting atmospheric response from such events regulates the geographic distribution of heat and cold, along with rain and snowfall.

A Modoki El Niño is a warming in the central equatorial rather than eastern equatorial region of the Pacific Ocean. A recent moderate Modoki El Niño in 2023 at the peak of solar cycle twenty-five contributed further to established global warming influences, while a subsequent La Niña along with gradually weakening solar ultraviolet warmth may have contributed to at least some transitory short term cooling. The influence of such patterns is most evident at mid latitudes across North America, Western Europe and the Asian countries of the Pacific Rim.

SPRING

MARCH 2025 Recent hurricane activity has notably altered the water temperatures of the Atlantic Ocean, which have risen to record levels in recent years. Consequently, late winter storm tracks along the East Coast of the United States are more ocean directed, leading to an increased chance for a brief late winter snowfall from the mid Atlantic states to New England. Deep South planting conditions are excellent this year. Still near the eleven-year solar maximum, mild days and cool nights from Florida to Texas bring ideal conditions. Colder than normal temperatures are felt through the Northern Plains, while the risk for a brief tornado outbreak near the end of the month emerges late in the month. Drier weather persists across the West Coast, though one Pacific Ocean born storm makes landfall by the twentieth. The storm has significant potential to make travel hazardous.

APRIL 2025 Coastal fog and cool east winds persist along coastal communities from Boston to Philadelphia. Spring arrives early this year with temperatures reaching the 70s, a daily occurrence from the Ohio Valley westward through the Great Plains. Most days are sunny in this region, with the promise of abundant crops soon following the arrival of welcome rainfall at months' end. The risk for severe thunderstorms and a tornado outbreak is heightened this year by La Niña conditions across the Central Plains. A brief late-season snowfall blankets northern Minnesota and North Dakota. Heavy snowfall occurs east of Salt Lake City and western Montana. The West Coast enjoys generally warm and dry days, although though one major storm brings wind and rain from central California to Seattle, with heavy snowfall blanketing the Sierra Nevada. North Texas and the rest of the Southern Plains receive a steady rainfall, essential for the arriving growing season. Florida enjoys sunny and warm weather.

MAY 2025 The growing season is off to a fast start at the peak of solar cycle 25. With the risk for hail producing thunderstorms increasing across the Central and Northern Plains, chances for such an event will occur at night under the influence of a lingering La Niña. Farther south, the weather turns dry, with ideal farming conditions. The lingering chill in New England eases with balmy days and cool nights. Afternoon seas breezes persist near the coast. Wet weather arrives across the mid Atlantic states and extends through the Carolinas. South of that wet weather pattern, hot and humid weather emerges from Georgia through Florida and west to New Orleans. Heat also builds in Arizona with first days of temperatures above 100 degrees felt in Phoenix.

SUMMER

JUNE 2025 As the Solstice arrives, so, too, ideal weather conditions for summer planting across northern states. Abundant Spring rainfall turns dry and warm with peak warmth from the Sun. Daily highs will average in the 70s with overnight lows in the 50s, A fast moving severe weather outbreak with strong winds and isolated hail will have minimal effect this early in the growing season.

A spectacular runoff season will greet hikers across the Rockies and California mountains, after abundant winter snowfall. Reservoirs are bank full while the growing season is supported by such conditions. During a time of generally dry weather in New England, scattered thunderstorms accompany two cold fronts between the first and fifteenth of the month. Hot and increasingly humid weather emerges across the Deep South. Late morning thunderstorms develop on Florida's East Coast with isolated convective storms later in the day from Tampa to Naples associated with afternoon sea breezes.

JULY 2025 Peak summer heat is persistent this year with only brief breaks of cooler air in New England and the Northern Plains east of the Rockies. The risk of night time thunderstorms runs high across the corn belt, resulting in some threat to yields there. Texas heat builds with risks to the power grid emerging again. Thunderstorms are more frequent from the Texas coast to Florida's West Coast. The first summer thunderstorms signal the beginning of the monsoon season through the mountainous West. Ocean water temperatures are above normal, signaling an active hurricane season ahead. Crop yields are bountiful this year with adequate Spring rainfall offsetting above normal temperatures in key growth areas.

AUGUST 2025 Tropical storm activity is likely to be above normal this year, occurring during a La Niña event or shortly thereafter. A concept called remnant vorticity involving the Sun causes the lingering influences of Pacific Ocean events to persist even after an El Niño and La Niña event has ended. Such "in between times" are called Las Nadas. In this instance, early season hurricanes are favored across the near Atlantic, close to the Florida coast and the Caribbean Sea. Summer heat reaches nationally, with above normal temperatures favored in New England, the Midwest and Southern Plains. Afternoon thunderstorms develop across the mountainous West, with a day of torrential downpours possible in Phoenix associated with a Pacific Ocean tropical storm near the coast of Mexico.

AUTUMN

SEPTEMBER 2025 Northern Atlantic Ocean water temperatures remain above normal and combined with the lingering effects of the La Niña ENSO event, this leaves the U.S. East Coast vulnerable to a landfalling hurricane this month. Specifically, New England and Florida are at greatest risk from such a storm. Conversely, unseasonably cold weather arrives across the mountainous West, along with an early frost in Montana and Wyoming. Across the Great Plains and Midwest, the harvest begins with dry conditions and near-drought conditions throughout Texas and Oklahoma. Locally heavy rains fall through the southern Rockies as Pacific Ocean tropical storm activity persists.

OCTOBER 2025 Hurricane activity eases across the Atlantic basin, with the risk for a late season landfalling storm limited to the Gulf Coast. Such a storm would bring relief from dry ground conditions to the Southern Plains. Thunderstorm activity eases in Florida with late morning isolated storms confined to the state's East Coast. Much of the month is dry nationally, while several Alberta Clippers deliver light rainfall from the Great Lakes and the Midwest through New England. Fall colors are especially bright this year, at the 11 year solar maximum and following substantial summer rainfall. Late in the month, the season's first snowfall dusts the Cascades and Sierra Nevada on the heels of an ocean born Pacific storm.

NOVEMBER 2025 Frost and freeze conditions become more widespread as an early season polar airmass sweeps the nation east of the Rockies. Rain squalls change to wet snow in western New York State. Sub-freezing temperatures are felt by the twentieth for major cities extending from Boston to Washington D.C. A fall coastal storm sweeps the East Coast with snow falling at higher elevations from West Virginia to New England. Fine fall weather is felt through much of the West, although several Pacific Coastal storms bring wind and rain from San Francisco to Seattle. Rain also falls briefly in Los Angeles. Florida enjoys dry and mild weather, though a strong cold front brings strong thunderstorms around Thanksgiving. Dry weather persists from the Midwest through the Great Plains.

WINTER

DECEMBER 2025 Meteorological Winter begins informally on December first, with cold and dry weather beginning the month. The early part of the month brings frigid temperatures, with lows below normal from the north central states eastward to New England. Further to the west, lake effect snows increase in western New York State and east of Lake Michigan. By mid month a fast moving arctic cold front brings the first light snowfalls from the Dakotas to New England. This is immediately followed in the Southern states by a surge of cold that reaches Texas and the Gulf States. Later in the month a storm emerges from the Gulf of Mexico bringing the best chance for a White Yule in years from New York City to Boston! The West Coast will be buffeted by several coastal storms. These will team up with wind-swept rain and mountain snows to produce a wet and chilly latter part of the month. Denver will also receive heavy snowfall which will extend to the South, covering Dallas.

JANUARY 2026 Easing warmth from the Sun and the lingering influence of La Niña are likely to bring noticeably milder midwinter conditions across the continental United States. The warm spell ends around the twentieth, with an east coast snowstorm delivering the coldest air of the year and markedly slowing air traffic. The entire region is impacted, but the Philadelphia corridor is especially vulnerable while snow also falls heavily east of the Great Lakes. At nearly the same time, a second storm channel is focused from Southern California through the Desert Southwest as rain even falls in Phoenix! Heavy snow falls on Salt Lake City and stretches throughout the intermountain West. The Pacific Northwest remains cool and dry though one storm threatens the region with heavy coastal rainfall and mountain snow.

FEBRUARY 2026 In the first part of the month, several intense storms sweep through the central and eastern United States from Chicago to Boston by the tenth. Heavy snow falls generally along the I-80 corridor although the immediate coastline is more likely to experience rainfall. Nevertheless, snowfall is likely to be above normal for most cities. Cold weather associated with such a storm track brings sub-freezing temperatures as far south as Florida, risking frost and threatening the citrus crop. Generally dry and cold weather persists across the Rockies even as heavy snow falls from northern New Mexico to Flagstaff and within the mountains east of Los Angeles. At the same time, wind and rain also arrive in San Francisco and Seattle.

PROTECTION AND THE SPIRIT WORLD

Protection is one of the main reasons for ritual tattooing. Many cultures believe people are vulnerable or more susceptible to evil forces through bodily orifices and feet as Djinn can try to enter the body through the Earth. Tattoos are put near those placements in order to prevent that. Berbers believe that a supernatural energy resides in all things and tattoos hold that sacred energy that could be used for many purposes. Their protection tattoos consist of mainly crosses, diamond or wheel designs applied while reciting *Quran* verses. These sort of designs are also used as a protection against the evil eye (tattoos are considered good for that because, as they are done with a sharp object, they pierce the evil eye,) and they are placed on the face near the eyes and on the hands.

The meaning of the cruciform elements, which are considered the best symbol by many, is that the symbol disperses the evil energy from the eye to all quarters of the earth on the winds, preventing from injuring the person looked at. These examples about prevention and protection from the evil eye come from Berber and Arab tattooing traditions, but there are numerous examples of tattoos produced with this same intention. They are frequently done in many cultures such as Bosnian Catholics or the Vlach.

There are many tattoo designs and beliefs regarding protection from Djinn and to aid in pregnancy because women were believed to be especially susceptible to their influence and they also get jealous of the sight of babies and try to cause miscarriage.

Some spirits don't like metal or sharp objects and the protective qualities of substances like lampblack and charcoal or urine, once tattooed in the body, kept the spirits away. It is very interesting that the same procedure that is used to repel some spirits and prevent possession is also used in the opposite way to facilitate the entrance of the spirit helper. Tattoos also help to 'hide' the wearer from those unwanted influences.

To protect the warriors and hunters, shamanic tattoos were done along with numerous prayers to make the recipient a sort of shapeshifter. Certain animals or animal markings would help the wearer become the animal and gain their strength and protection in their journeys, like Labret tattoos imitating the markings of orcas.

—ROSA LAGUNA

Leechdoms and Wortcunning and Starcraft, Oh My!

The Lacnunga, The Leechbook and
Anglo Saxon Herbal Charms and Galdor

ᚠᚢᚦᚨᚱᚲᚷᚹᚾᛁᛃᛁᛟᛋᛏᚤ

Remember, Wormwood, what thou didst reveal. What thou didst prepare at the great proclamation. Una thou art named, the eldest of herbs; Thou art strong against three and against thirty, Thou art strong against venom and against infection. Thou art strong against the Evil Thing that goes throughout the land.

And thou. Plantain, mother of herbs, Open from the east, mighty within. Over thee carts creaked, queens rode over thee, Over thee brides made cries, bulls gnashed over thee.

All those thou didst withstand and dashed against them; So mayst thou withstand venom and infection And the Evil Thing that goes throughout the land.

Water-cress is this herb named; it grew on stone. It stands against venom, it fights against pain.

Nettle is this called; it dashes against venom. It drives away cruel things, it casts out venom. This is the herb that fought with the snake; This is strong against venom, this is strong against infection. This is strong against the Evil Thing that goes throughout the land.

Fly now, Betonica, the less from the greater. The greater from the less, till there be to them a cure for both.

Remember, Camomile, what thou didst make known. What thou didst bring to pass at Alorford, That for the flying ill he never yielded up his life After one prepared Camomile for him to eat.

This is the herb that is called Wild-Apple. The seal sent this over the back of the sea, To heal the hurt of other venom.

These nine attacked nine venoms.

A serpent came sneaking; he slew a man. Then took Woden nine glory-twigs, Smote the serpent then so that it flew in nine pieces; There the apple ended it and its venom, So that it never would enter house again.

Thyme and Fennel, two exceeding mighty ones, These herbs the wise Lord made, Holy in the heavens; He let them down, Placed them and sent them into the seven worlds As a cure for all, the poor and the rich. It stands against pain, it dashes against venom, It is strong against three and against thirty, Against the hand of an enemy and against the hand of the cursed…And against the bewitching of my creatures.

Now these nine herbs are strong against nine curse things, against nine venoms and against nine infections: against the red venom, against the gray venom, against the white venom, against the blue venom, against the 50 yellow venom, against the green venom, against the black venom, against the brown venom, against the purple venom; against snake-blister, against water-blister, against thorn-blister, against thistle-blister, against ice-blister, against poison-blister;

If any venom come flying from the east, or if any come from the north, or any from the west over the people. Christ stood over venom of every kind.

Mugwort, way-bread, nettle, crab-apple, thyme and fennel, the elder soap-plant. Pound these herbs into dust, mix with soap and with apple-dirt. Make into a paste with water and ashes, take fennel and wool into the paste and bathe it with beaten eggs, then make it into a salve, either before or after. Sing this spell upon all of the herbs—three times before one makes it and also upon the apples—and sing for the men by mouth and into their ear both and into the wound that same spell, before one applies that salve.

tr. Thomas Oswald Cockayne

ANGLO-SAXON herbals are invaluable sources of knowledge that offer insights into the medicinal and magical properties of plants in the Anglo-Saxon period. These herbals, such as the *Lacnunga and the Leechbook*, provide a wealth of information about the identification, preparation and uses of various herbs for healing purposes. They reflect the deep connection between the Anglo-Saxons and the natural world, as well as their understanding of the therapeutic properties of different plants. These herbals not only serve as windows into the medical practices of the time but also offer glimpses into the magical beliefs and spiritual traditions surrounding herbal medicine showcasing the profound significance of plants in the daily lives of the Anglo-Saxons.

Chief among these early texts is the *Lacnunga*, a collection of Old English texts, holds a treasure trove of knowledge about ancient healing and magical practices. Compiled during the tenth century, this manuscript is a snap shot of the overall traditions of the Anglo-Saxons. The *Lacnunga* continues to captivate researchers and enthusiasts alike.

The well known philologist Thomas Oswald Cockayne collected and illumined with analysis the *Lacnunga*. While not actually a separate book, this was the title afforded a look by Cockayne to a section of medical scripts and charms whose origins point to a much earlier era of knowledge.

Content and Structure

The *Lacnunga* is a compilation of various texts, many of which focus on medical treatments, charms and incantations. It is believed to have been assembled by

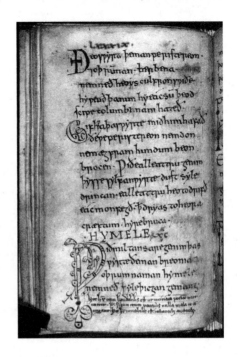

Extracted page from the Lacnunga

a scribe who combined older texts with new additions. The manuscripts consist of a mixture of Latin and Old English, reflecting the linguistic context of the time.

One of the most well-known sections of the *Lacnunga* is the "Nine Herbs Charm" (excerpted at the at the beginning of this article,) a remarkable text that describes a remedy for various ailments using a combination of medicinal plants. The first two thirds of this piece enumerate the herbs to be used, glossing the magical properties of each. The last third is the instructions for preparations for using them both physically and magically.

Another significant portion of the *Lacnunga* is the "Leechbook," a compilation of medical recipes and treatments. It covers a wide range of condi-

Extracted spread from Bald's Leechbook

tions, including fractures, skin diseases and even supernatural afflictions. The Leechbook reveals the intricate knowledge of the Anglo-Saxon healers and their practical approach to medicine. While some of the remedies may seem peculiar by today's standards, they reflect the cultural and scientific understanding of the time.

Magical Practices

In addition to its medical content, the *Lacnunga* also contains charms and incantations that were believed to possess magical properties. These texts, often referred to as "wyrd," were recited to bring about desired outcomes or protect against evil forces. They were considered an essential part of everyday life, with rituals and beliefs intertwined with the fabric of society.

The charms in the *Lacnunga* often draw upon a blend of Christian and Pagan elements, reflecting the cultural

syncretism of the Anglo-Saxon period. They provide insight into the complex religious and spiritual beliefs held by the people of that time. Whether invoking the power of Christ or calling upon the aid of Pagan deities, these charms demonstrate the diverse tapestry of faith that existed in Anglo-Saxon England.

Significance and Legacy

The *Lacnunga* holds immense significance for understanding Anglo-Saxon culture, spirituality and medical practices. It provides a window into a bygone era, shedding light on the lives and beliefs of the ancestors. Through its diverse content, it allows for the exploration of the ancient healing techniques, the power of language through magical incantation and the interconnectedness of the natural and supernatural realms.

The impact of the manuscript extends well beyond the realm of academia. The *Lacnunga* has inspired contemporary practitioners of herbal medicine who seek to understand the historical roots of their craft. It has also influenced modern Pagans and magical practitioners, who find resonance in the ancient charms and rituals preserved within its pages.

Lacnunga vs Culpeper

The *Lacnunga* and Culpeper's herbal writings are two distinct sources that provide insights into different time periods and cultural contexts.

The *Lacnunga*, as previously discussed, is an Old English manuscript compiled during the tenth century. It primarily focuses on healing practices, magical charms and medical treatments of the Anglo-Saxon period. It offers a glimpse into the beliefs and traditions of the Anglo-Saxons, their use of plants for healing and their intertwining of Christian and Pagan elements in their charms and rituals. The *Lacnunga* reflects the cultural and spiritual context of the Anglo-Saxon era and provides valuable information about their medical and magical practices.

On the other hand, Culpeper's herbal writings belong to a later period in history. Nicholas Culpeper was a seventeenth century English physician and herbalist who published a renowned herbal guide called *The English Physician*" Culpeper's writings focus on the medicinal properties and uses of plants according to the humoral theory prevalent during his time. He aimed to make herbal medicine accessible to the common people by translating Latin medical texts into English and providing practical advice for using herbs to treat various ailments.

While the *Lacnunga* showcases the beliefs and practices of the ancient Anglo-Saxons, Culpeper's writings reflect the evolving medical knowledge and cultural context of the seventeenth century. Culpeper's approach is more influenced by the emerging scientific understanding of the time, while the *Lacnunga* encompasses a broader spectrum of magical and spiritual elements associated with herbal medicine.

Both the *Lacnunga* and Culpeper's writings contribute valuable information to the study of herbal medicine, but they offer distinct perspectives from different historical periods. The *Lacnunga* provides insights into the ancient Anglo-Saxon worldview and their use of herbs in healing and magic, while Culpeper's writings offer a glimpse into the evolving understanding and practical applications of herbs during the seventeenth century.

Conclusion

The *Lacnunga* stands as a remarkable testament to the wisdom, beliefs and practices of the Anglo-Saxons. Its contents provide a fascinating glimpse into a time when healing, magic and spirituality were intricately woven into the fabric of daily life. Through its medical recipes, charms and incantations, the *Lacnunga* serves as a bridge between the past and the present, allowing us to appreciate the rich cultural heritage of the ancestors. Its enduring legacy continues to captivate and inspire scholars and enthusiasts, a reminder of the enduring power of ancient knowledge.

—DEMETRIUS SANTIAGO

THE SOUND OF SILENCE

IN THE NATURAL world, there is a conversation circulating around that most people are unaware of. To become conscious of it, you need to pause and listen, though not with your ears—with your heart. Only then shall you hear the language of the animal, plant and mineral kingdoms, to which, of course, humans essentially belong. In order to participate in this soundless conversation, nothing more is required than to pause, be still and listen.

In the long struggle to survive, human beings have confronted—and indeed still do confront—enormous natural challenges. So, too, in their own way, have all forms of life. However, as rational beings, humans have grown increasingly detached from the natural world, bereft of that intuitive feeling of being a part of it. Above all, humanity has forgotten how to listen. Instead, filled with the notion of separateness and distracted by their busy little lives, people remain deaf to the conversations going on throughout nature. They remain deaf to what—in the words of Madame Blavatsky—is the voice of the silence. Yet you have only to pause and be still, reflecting not on your separateness but on the mysterious togetherness that embraces all of creation, to hear for the first time the conversation going on around you. You thereby become yourself a part of it.

In the depths of a forest or on a clifftop overlooking the sea, or, come to that, even in your own backyard, you can learn how to participate with little effort in that wordless conversation which you were a fully conscious part of at one time. Herein lies the secret of magical practice—its effectiveness is derived from the fundamental unity behind the superficial diversity of form. The techniques may vary. Ritual—whether simple or elaborate—is but the means to an end and those obsessed with formalities are least likely to get to that end. The Gods and Goddesses are representative of subtle forces that express themselves in nature and will not be bothered by how you look, what you wear, or even if you sometimes get their names wrong. You are, after all, only human.

The secret language of Nature is secret only because people seldom pause to listen. By listening you rediscover your place both in this world and in the subtle world beyond it. Just as you learn as an occultist to behold Nature with the eye of the heart, so you must learn to listen with the ear of the soul. Here is your chance to be once again part of the conversation.

You are made of stardust, as indeed is everything else, animate and inanimate alike. This means all are interconnected, each of you attuned like a spider at the centre of her web to the world around yourself. Every breath you take mingles with the subtle respiration of each blade of grass, of each plant and of every tree. You need only pause, be still and calmly listen to become aware of that all-pervading consciousness of which you and everything else are a part. Truly yourself and at one again with your surroundings, you shall finally have hearkened to the sound of silence. None other is more sublime.

—NINA FALAISE

The Three Ghostly Ladies Of Pluckley

THE ANCIENT village of Pluckley lies approximately twenty-five miles from Canterbury in the county of Kent. Deemed the most haunted village in England in 1989 by the Guinness Book of World Records, this charming yet unassuming hamlet has an embarrassment of ghosts. They are all connected to the Dering Baronetcy, its seat Surrenden Dering, the thirteenth century church of St. Nicholas and Greystones Manor. Surrenden was more than partially destroyed by fire in 1952 but St. Nicholas and Greystones are still intact and an integral part of the village along with Rose Court. Just why there are so many ghosts in Pluckley is unclear, but no less than fifteen spectres—including the screaming man, the highwayman and the old gypsy woman—are said to reside alongside the 1,000 living souls of this parish. This tale will concentrate, however, on the Red Lady, the White Lady and the Lady of Rose Court. These feminine apparitions are reminiscent of the three graces, the three Fates, the three Witches of Macbeth, the Graeae and the Gorgons of old.

Buried in St Nicholas, Lady Dering—the Red Lady of Pluckley—haunts the cemetery and crypt. She was only twenty-three when she died during the summer of her youth. Her husband the Baron wanted to preserve her great beauty so he arranged for her to be buried with a red rose in a three-layered coffin to slow down the decomposition. This did not confine her, however. It is said that she died in childbirth, giving birth to a still-born child and this is why she haunts the graveyard today, looking for her lost baby.

Thought to be a relative of Baroness Dering, the White Lady haunts the inside of St Nicholas' Church. White Ladies are seen all over the world, typically in rural areas associated with local legends of tragedy. Common to many of these legends is an accidental death, murder or suicide, along with the themes of loss, betrayal and unrequited love.

In popular folklore, White Ladies are fabled to appear by day as well as by night in houses in which a family member is soon to die. In line with this, Pluckley's White Lady was also seen in the library of Surrenden Dering before the blaze of 1952. It was the site of the U.S. Embassy between the wars and her apparition was said to be seen by multiple staff. One employee even held an all-night vigil on Christmas Eve to catch a sighting of the lady and when she did eventually appear, he attempted to shoot her spectral form with his rifle. The shot apparently passed straight through her apparition and disappeared into the panelled wall—to a tunnel that led towards St. Nicholas.

The third and final member of the triumvirate is the Lady of Rose Court. Thought to be a mistress of one of the Dering family, the Lady may also have become entangled in a love triangle with the Miserable Monk of Greystones. The pair had stolen moments of romance in the little lanes near the village, but the affair was destined to end tragically. Unable to stand the pressure, she committed suicide by eating poisonous berries. She haunts the house and the gardens between four and five in the afternoon, when it is said she can be heard calling for her two dogs, Penelope and Greenacre. Shortly after she died, the unhappy monk perished of a broken heart, and his pitiful spirit now wanders the gardens of Greystones. Perhaps one day their spirits will meet and they can wander the lanes again together.

—SARAH SIMPSON

YEMỌJA

The Yoruba All Mother

THE YORÙBÁ people of Southwestern Nigeria have long held deep reverence for a group of deities called Òrisá, which are considered direct emanations of Olódùmarè, the primordial foundation of all creation. These deities serve as intermediaries through which humans can connect with the divine. Among the most venerated of the Irúnmolè is Yemọja, often revered as the Mother of All Waters. Yemọja embodies nurturing, fertility and the sustenance of life, offering a profound connection to the mysteries of creation and the maternal forces of nature. Throughout their history, the Yoruba people have aspired to a deeper understanding of both the divine and the natural world. The Yoruba pantheon has recognized and embraced the dual nature of divine forces, both creative and destructive, striving to understand the relationship between the mundane and the spiritual.

Building upon this rich tradition, Yemọja's influence extends far beyond the borders of West Africa. As the Yoruba people were dispersed across the globe through the transatlantic slave trade, Yemọja, known also as Yemaya in the Americas, became a vital figure in Afro-descendant spiritual practices. Her attributes of motherhood and the nurturing essence of water resonated deeply with these communities, providing a source of comfort and resilience in the face of immense hardship. Yemọja/Yemaya's worship evolved as it adapted to new cultural contexts, blending with local traditions and beliefs, yet retaining the core aspects of her nurturing and protective nature. The multifaceted aspects of Yemọja/Yemaya will be explored, including her significance within Yoruba religious practices, her adaptation in diasporic contexts and the fascinating intersections between these perspectives.

Yoruba Perspectives

Within Yoruba cosmology, Yemọja holds a place of utmost importance, often depicted as the mother of all Orishas and primarily associated with fresh waters such as rivers and lakes. Her domain includes these bodies of water, making her a central figure in rituals associated with purification, fertility and healing. The name Yemọja is derived from the Yoruba words *Yeye omo eja*, which means "Mother whose children are fish," highlighting her nurturing and protective nature. Yemọja is revered as a compassionate mother who nurtures and protects her children with unwavering love and guidance.

Yemọja is revered as the Goddess of the Ogun River, which flows past the significant cities of Oyo and Abeokuta in Nigeria. This river, integral to the lives of the Yoruba people, is imbued with her nurturing and protective essence. The Ogun River is not only sacred to Yemọja but is also associated with other deities. For instance, Oshun, another prominent Orisha, is connected to the Oshun River, a tributary of the Ogun River, symbolizing love, beauty and fertility. These deities coexist within the Yoruba pantheon, each embodying distinct yet complementary aspects of the natural world and human experience, highlighting the intricate spiritual landscape that Yemọja and her fellow Orishas inhabit.

Yemọja is renowned for her motherhood of the powerful Orishas Sango and Ogun. Sango, the Orisha of thunder, lightning and fire, is celebrated for his fierce warrior spirit and commanding presence. He is the son of Yemọja and Orungan, who is also associated with the winds and the sky. Ogun, the Orisha of iron, warfare and labor, is revered for his strength, craftsmanship and tireless dedication and his father is Orunmila, the Orisha of wisdom and divination. As their mother, Yemọja nurtured and guided them, instilling in them the values of courage, resilience and responsibility. Despite their formidable powers and occasional conflicts, Yemọja's unwavering love and wisdom played a crucial role in shaping their destinies. Her nurturing influence is evident in their legacies, as both Sango and Ogun are integral to the Yoruba spiritual tradition, embodying the complex interplay of protection, creation and destruction that defines the human experience.

The Arugba Osun. She is charged with carrying the igba Yemoja in Osogbo during Yemoja's festival.

In Oyo and other regions of Yorubaland, festivals and ritual practices dedicated to Yemoja are grand events marked by vibrant activities and deep communal participation. During the annual Yemoja Festival, worshippers gather along riverbanks, particularly those of the Ogun River, to celebrate and honor the Goddess. The ceremonies begin with a procession to the water's edge, where priests and priestesses lead the community in chants and prayers, invoking Yemoja's presence and blessings.

Participants often dress in flowing blue and white garments, symbolizing Yemoja's connection to water. The rhythmic beats of drums fill the air, accompanied by the melodic sounds of traditional songs praising Yemoja.

Dancers perform intricate movements that mimic the flow and waves of the river, embodying the Goddess's nurturing and protective essence.

Ritual activities include the casting of offerings such as flowers and other symbolic items into the river to appease Yemoja and seek her favor. Devotees may also engage in spiritual cleansing rituals, submerging themselves partially in the water to wash away negative energies and renew their spiritual strength.

Throughout the festival, storytelling sessions recount the myths and legends of Yemoja, reinforcing her importance and the moral lessons embedded in her tales. The festival often culminates in a dramatic reenactment of significant events from Yemoja's mythology, providing a vivid

A Lucumi igba (sacred container) for Yemoja.

connection between the community and their spiritual heritage. This immersive experience fosters a sense of unity and continuity, ensuring that the reverence for Yemọja remains a vital part of Yoruba cultural identity.

Yoruba religious practices dedicated to Yemọja are rich and elaborate, involving intricate ceremonies, offerings, songs and dances. Altars dedicated to her worship are adorned with her sacred colors, blue and white, creating a visually striking and spiritually potent space. These altars often feature an array of meaningful objects, such as small river-worn stones, sixteen cowry shells through which she speaks and a pot of water from the river, which is refreshed each morning to maintain its purity and connection to Yemọja.

Large wooden statues depicting Yemọja are prominently placed on the altar, embodying her presence and providing a focal point for worship. These statues are paraded during her festivals, carried through the community to the rhythm of drums and chants, allowing all to share in the veneration.

The water from the altar is also used in significant rituals, such as anointing newborns, symbolizing Yemọja's blessing and protection over their lives. The combination of these elements creates a rich tapestry of worship, deeply connecting devotees to the nurturing and protective essence of Yemọja.

Offerings such as fruits, sweets, blue Chrysanthemum flowers, pounded yam, yam porridge, goats, hens and ducks are presented to Yemọja to appease her benevolent spirit and seek her blessings for protection, prosperity and emotional well-being. These offerings are placed on her altars and presented with deep reverence during ceremonies, accompanied by songs and dances that honor her nurturing and protective nature.

Yemọja has specific taboos that her devotees strictly observe. Dogs and okra leaves are forbidden in rituals dedicated to her, as they are considered impure and disrespectful to her essence. Additionally, in some areas where Yemọja's worship overlaps with that of Sango, his taboos are also observed out of respect for their close connection. This includes avoiding certain foods and practices that are prohibited in Sango's rituals, ensuring harmony and reverence in the shared spiritual landscape.

Myths

The mythology surrounding Yemọja is replete with tales that highlight her nurturing nature and fierce protective instincts. She is depicted as both a gentle mother who cares for her children and a powerful deity capable of unleashing storms and tidal waves when provoked or dishonored. In this duality lies the complexity of her character, embodying both gentleness and strength, mercy and wrath.

In one particular story, Yemọja's marriage to Oranmiyan, a legendary figure in Yoruba history and the founder of the Oyo Empire, is rich with emotional depth and significance. Their union held great promise, blending Yemọja's nurturing nature with Oranmiyan's leadership and strength. However, the marriage was marked by discord and challenges. Oranmiyan's demanding role as a ruler and warrior often kept him away from home, causing strain in their relationship. Eventually, the differences and pressures proved too great, leading to Yemoja's departure. Heartbroken but resolute, she gathered her sacred pots of water and left Oranmiyan. Realizing she was gone, Oranmiyan gave chase to convince her to return. As Yemoja retreated, the waters in her pots spilled and became the Ogun River. This departure not only underscored her independence and resilience but also reinforced her deep connection to the life-giving and nurturing forces of nature.

One of the most renowned stories associated with Yemoja centers around her role as the mother of Ogun, the Orisha of iron and warfare and the struggles she faced in raising him. According to legend, Ogun was a fiercely independent and headstrong child who often challenged his mother's authority. Despite their occasional conflicts, Yemo ja remained steadfast in her love for Ogun, guiding him with compassion and wisdom as he embarked on his journey as a warrior and protector of the community.

Following her departure from Oranmiyan, Yemoja eventually entered into a subsequent marriage with Okere, another significant figure in Yoruba mythology. Unlike her previous union, this relationship was marked by severe discord and turbulence. Okere—known for his volatile temper and impulsive nature—often clashed with Yemoja's serene and nurturing disposition. In one notable incident, Okere made a disparaging comment about Yemoja's breasts, further fueling the tension between them. This particular affront was the final straw for Yemoja. In a moment of desperation and anger, she invoked her powers to protect herself, transforming Okere into a rock as a stark reminder of the consequences of unchecked fury and disrespect. Subsequently, it became a tradition for the chiefs of the town to cover their faces when crossing the Ogun River, as a sign of respect and acknowledgment of the incident. This marriage further emphasized Yemoja's strength and independence, as well as her unwavering commitment to maintaining peace and harmony in her domain.

Diasporic Adaptations

The transatlantic slave trade forcibly dispersed millions of Yorubas from their homeland, leading to the preservation and adaptation of Yoruba religious traditions in the Americas. Yemoja/Yemaya, along with other Orishas, found new life in the diaspora, undergoing syncretism with Catholicism and indigenous beliefs to survive persecution and maintain spiritual practices.

In Afro-Cuban and Afro-Brazilian religions such as Santería/Lucumí and Candomblé, Yemoja is worshipped under various syncretic identities, often fused with Catholic saints such as Our Lady of Regla or the Virgin Mary. These syncretic manifestations allowed enslaved Africans to continue their worship clandestinely while outwardly conforming to the dominant religion imposed by colonial powers.

In the diaspora, Yemọja/Yemaya's attributes expanded to encompass not only her original roles as a water deity but also broader aspects of femininity, motherhood and protection. She is closely associated with the ocean and the deity Olokun in both Lucumí and Candomblé traditions. She became a symbol of resilience and survival for Afro-descendant communities facing oppression and marginalization, offering solace and empowerment to those who sought her guidance.

Intersections and Continuities

The relationship between Yemọja in Yoruba tradition and her diasporic adaptations reveals a dynamic interplay of continuity and transformation. Core attributes and rituals remain consistent, yet there are notable shifts driven by historical, social and environmental factors. In the Americas, rituals honoring Yemọja may incorporate local cultural elements, reflecting the experiences of the diaspora. Her symbolism also evolves to address contemporary issues like environmental degradation, social justice and gender equality.

Despite these adaptations, Yemọja's essence as a nurturing and protective force endures, unifying Yoruba spirituality with its diasporic expressions. Whether worshipped on the shores of Nigeria or the streets of Havana, her presence continues to inspire reverence, resilience and renewal among her devotees.

Yemọja occupies a sacred space in Yoruba cosmology and its diasporic extensions, embodying timeless qualities of femininity, fertility and the life-giving force of water. Across continents and

Candomble statue of Yemọja

centuries, her followers find solace, strength and spiritual sustenance in her enduring presence, adapting her worship to meet the challenges of changing times and contexts.

In navigating the complexities of identity, culture and spirituality in an increasingly interconnected world, Yemọja serves as a potent symbol of resilience, continuity and the enduring power of ancestral wisdom. Whether invoked in traditional rituals or contemporary ceremonies, her essence transcends borders and boundaries, reminding humanity of shared connections and the eternal flow of life's waters.

—IFADOYIN SANGOMUYIWA

Yemoja, ìyá omo èrò,
Ìyá agbàlá ayé,
Òrìsá tó ń gbé l'ódò,
Ìyá gbogbo omo omi.

Mo júbà fún Yemoja,
Òrìsá tó ń sún omi,
E se, ìyá, alàáàánú,
Kí a má rí ibi, kí a má subú.

Yemoja, mother of many children,
Mother who nurtures the world,
Òrìsá who dwells in the river,
Mother of all water beings.

I pay homage to Yemoja,
Òrìsá who moves within the waters,
Thank you, mother, full of compassion,
May we not encounter evil, may we not fall.

–traditional praise poetry for Yemoja

The Statue of Peace at Nagasaki Peace Park

An inscription at the base in Japanese translates to "This is our cry. This is our prayer. For building peace in this world." These words serve as a poignant reminder of the devastating consequences of war and the importance of striving for peace and reconciliation.

MEN OF THE CRAFT
SACRED MASCULINITY AND THE WILD MAN MYTHOS

Vetting the Sacred Masculine

Martin Schongauer engraving: "Shield with a Greyhound, Held by a Wild Man" (1490.) Here the wild man's stance and gaze might be suggestive of being captured or trapped, perhaps despairing over having been confined—or even tamed.

Sometimes a wild god comes to the table.

He is awkward and does not know the ways,

Of porcelain, of fork, and mustard, and silver.

His voice makes vinegar from wine,

And brings the dead to life.

–TOM HIRONS, *Sometimes a Wild God*

MUCH OF WHAT presents as masculinity in western culture today is considered anything but sacred. For several decades, the male principle has largely been deemed toxic, a perspective that impacts men throughout their lives and in their relationships and roles as fathers, husbands, partners, brothers and more. The result is the continuation of a growing spiritual and generational divide, with men experiencing personal disconnection from Self and often lacking a strong, healthy community with other men, in addition to being disconnected from familial and ancestral bonds and—

predictively—those generations that will follow.

In the growing wake of evolving and often ambiguous social and gender roles, men are continuing to seek authenticity and self-empowerment in the sense of that primal maleness untouched and unfettered by the conflicting demands and expectations of a patriarchal worldview and the reemerging Divine Feminine. With respect to women and the Divine Feminine, women have been subjugated, dismissed and ultimately compelled to hold ground and respond *en force* to generalized male toxicity manifesting as the deficiency or imbalance of the Sacred Masculine in the guise of patriarchy. While the Goddess has been returning to western consciousness through the women's movement, feminist scholarship and reawakening and rise of the Divine Feminine, what is not acknowledged is that the Sacred Masculine has similarly suffered and been forced underground by centuries of religious dogma, political conflict and conflicting social norms that sought to suppress, dominate or debase the core masculine principle.

The Wild(er) Man of the Craft

The medieval mythos of the Wild Man recounts the perils—both physical and spiritual—that existed for those marginalized individuals or social groups who were compelled to live outside the bounds of civilization or who otherwise rejected mainstream religious and social structure. In his essay "Wild Men and Spain's Brave New World" in the classic compilation *Wild Man Within*, Stanley Robe said, "the Wild Man has been discussed in Freudian terms as representative of the potentialities lurking in the heart of every individual, whether primitive or civilized, as his possible incapacity" (or reluctance?) "to come to terms with his socially provided

world." Considered touched by madness but imbued with physical power and sexual potency, the Wild Man existed in a feral or natural state at odds with the civilized world and its constituents. Like the mythical satyrs and wild Gods before him, the Wild Man was exemplified by his strength and fecundity—as well as his resoluteness and perseverance in the face of adversity as civilization increasingly encroached on the natural world.

Perhaps now more than at any time in history men find themselves increasingly as outsiders, often deciding or forced to reject originally familiar and mainstream but now continually evolving social or gender conventions to forge unique identities and occupy increasingly diverse roles. Lives are in perpetual motion—if not upheaval or even conflict—from one event or place to the next. From cradle to grave there are rarely, if any, recognizable rites of passage that mark major life transitions and men are often left to navigate their way without the guidance and support of other men or of an established, long-term community.

In *Permission to be a Man*, transformational coach Heinrich Resenhoffer suggests that men, "have lost the lineage of the sacred masculine in our modern society of men teaching men how to be men, love between men, men passing on the ancient wisdom of men, men holding the space for men, men calling other men out when they break their sacred contracts of manhood." Men of the Craft might find themselves largely solitary, being not only removed from or discouraged from community practice but reminded that they are considered outsiders or otherwise unwelcome in a

largely feminine, Goddess-centric Craft or Pagan community.

It's time to redefine and resurrect the Sacred Masculine for the benefit of men—and not merely that the Goddess may have a proper consort. The answer to balancing the Divine Feminine and the Sacred Masculine is not by sway of a fulcrum which operates on subjective principle but by elimination of a false dichotomy profiteered by New Age practitioners and spiritual coaches within the Craft and healing communities. There is no duality implied when men must acknowledge and heal their divine feminine half. Ultimately, men must find and take back their voices and work toward their own healing and the healing of other men, just as women must do for other women.

—LOREN CRAWFORD

You Don't Know Jack!

WHO IS this character Jack that we have all grown up with, but really don't know? Jack climbs a beanstalk, nimbly jumps over a candlestick, climbs a hill with his best friend Jill, sits in a corner and is frosty in the coldest winter months. Jack is in a pulpit, gives his name to a lighted pumpkin and adorns the flag of the British Empire. Exactly who is Jack?

The name Jack is a popularized form of John, the French Jacques, which is equivalent of Jacob and James, and is also a nickname for Jacob. While many of the older nursery rhymes featuring Jack are of English origin, some go much further back and may have several occult meanings. The

story of Jack and the Beanstalk, for example, is an English fairy tale written in 1734 as "The Story of Jack Spriggins and the Enchanted Bean." Research by Durham University and the NOVA University of Lisbon indicates the story may have originated as far back as 4,500 to 2,500 BCE as a genre in which a boy steals an ogre's treasure and might also have Proto-Indo-Iranian roots. Utilizing the Jack nickname of Jacob brings to mind the biblical story of Jacob's Ladder, reaching high into the heavens to see the face of God. Jacob's Ladder is also symbolic of the spine and Kundalini energy which climbs up through chakras from the root to the crown towards enlightenment. Jack is ambitious!

The story of Jack and Jill climbing a hill and then falling down with a head injury could have several meanings. An Icelandic tale from *Gylfaginning*—the thirteenth century Old Norse *Prose Edda*—details a story about Hjúki and his sister Bil, who were stolen by the Moon while drawing water from a well, and can still be seen on the Moon's face to this day. More humble interpretations include a local girl who became pregnant and the responsible father who died from a rockfall, the executions of Richard Empson and Edmund Dudley in 1514 or a satire of King Charles I of England's attempt to reduce the volume of a Jack—an eighth of a pint—while keeping the tax the same.

Jack Be Nimble, Jack Be Quick is most likely symbolic of jumping candlesticks without extinguishing the flame, which was considered good luck to do and was also a form of divination. Little Jack Horner Sitting in a Corner is another English nursery rhyme from the eighteenth century mainly concerning opportunistic politics of the day.

The very flag of the United Kingdom is named after Jack—or is it? The Union Jack consists of the combined flags of England and Scotland since the regal union in 1606, with a red cross on a white background known as St. George's Cross for England and a white X-shaped St. Andrew's Cross on a blue background for Scotland. For this flag, the Union Jack was a shortening of Jacobus—the Latin version

of James—for King James VI and I. However, the name Jack in the context of flagstaffs and maritime colors also refers to the smaller ensign used to identify ship's nationality, as well as the staff or pole to hang them from. "You are alsoe for this present service to keepe in your Boultspritt end and your Pendant and your Ordinance." Basically, His Majesty's ships were to fly small jack flags from the bowsprit and the large Union Jack on the main or stern.

In natural settings, Jack can be seen as the spadix which is nearly enclosed in the Jack-in-the-pulpit flowering plant family of Araceae. Jackrabbits cover numerous species of hares found throughout the Americas, Eurasia and Africa.

Everyone's favorite holiday decoration—the jack-o'-lantern—has a darker tale that the candlelight hides well. The name comes from the

phenomenon of strange lights flickering over peat bogs, also known as will-o'-the-wisps. As a side note, these bog lights are natural, caused by the oxidation of phosphine, diphosphane and methane from organic decay. The jack-o'-lantern common today originated with grotesquely carved root vegetables such as turnips or rutabaga, which produced a realistic human head due to their shapes. Adding small candles inside them produced a small lantern. Folktales add to the darker side of lighted pumpkin faces, as recalled from *The Legend of Sleepy Hollow* by Washing Irving, whose Headless Horseman chases Ichabod Crane. A better tale from Ireland tells of Stingy Jack, a blacksmith who loses a bet with the Devil and must spend eternity wandering the land between Heaven and Hell, using a jack-o'-lantern as his light source at night.

Finally, Jack Frost as the personification of wintry forecasts and the hardening of all things water causes all to suffer from chilly noses and frostbitten toes. A younger version of Old Man Winter, Jack Frost evokes a colder version of Loki, the Norse God of mischief. Jack Frost and Loki are both regarded as malicious and beneficial, depending upon one's perspective. Jack Frost playfully paints the natural world and windows with strokes of frost, icicles and snowflakes, ultimately causing the death of the summer months to allow nature to sleep and regenerate for another season. Seen as a woodland sprite or a sinister character in modern culture, Jack Frost is the ultimate Jack characterization as he owns a quarter of the year for most people, who try to stay warm until he finally flies away and leaves us alone—for a while.

JOHN NUTTALL

109

SÁMI DRUM SPIRITS

Allies for a Different Time?

THE NOAIDI are the traditional indigenous shamans of the Sámi people living in arctic Scandinavia and are related to some Siberians. Sámi reindeer herders and their now semi-nomadic lifestyle have long captivated imagination and interest, their shamanic based magics the most. Despite prejudice, oppression and submission, the Sámi have remained buoyant enough to embrace a revitalisation of their traditions and customs that began over a decade ago and is thriving still. Although the Sámi today largely adhere to the teachings of the Lutheran Church, they seek the fulfilment of reciprocal ancestral tradition.

Rediscovering the roots of ones' people and finding the threads of lore and custom is an arduous but not a thankless task. All things shift in time, making them relevant and relatable to a whole new generation of people who live in a very different world. Today, tourism has impacted the world of the Sámi and the crafting traditions of their ancestral heritage have adapted to accommodate the increasing interest in the spiritual and magical traditions that remain unique in the modern world. Communing still with the spirits of the land, sea and air, they celebrate again a culture that resounds through song (*yoiking*), icon and drum (*runebomme*—the shamanic vehicle).

During the Witch hysteria of the seventeenth to nineteenth centuries, priests and missionaries across Lapland sought to eradicate Sámi religious practices through high taxation, corporal punishment and death sentences. During this cultural upheaval, hundreds of Noaidi rune-bommes were confiscated and burned by priests who saw them as tools for summoning the devil. Other drums were distributed around the world for display in museums or for private collectors. Only 71 drums remain. Sámi people of today are painstakingly correcting the many errors attached to the symbolism of their magics as they, too, rediscover their meanings, made ever more complex because the beliefs held by the Sámi differ somewhat between regions and tribes.

Shamanism is perhaps the least understood praxis of a fading world. Within the holistic world of the Sámi, everything is deemed sacred. Everything houses a spirit that can be propitiated, coaxed into guidance and assistance by the Noaidi whose role as spiritual inter-mediators is vital for community well-being. Noaidi are guided and taught by *Sáivu* (underworld) spirits to mediate spirit, to navigate the worlds and to be the memory of the Sámi people. They are the keepers of cultural heritage through song (yoiks) and storytelling. Yoiking induces trance—it is a calling of the spirits rather like the Scandinavian Varðlokkur as well as a method of spell casting. Adapted for the modern world by a younger generation, the yoik has been brought up to date, accompanied now with folk and rock music. More traditional forms of the yoik resembled low mumblings and demonstrate the unintelligible chants associated with spell craft. Yoiks may also mimic natural sounds of the elements and of animals.

Noaidi drums were—and are once again—tools used to assist out-of-body trance journeys, vision quests, healing, soul retrieval, prophecy and divination. Sámi cosmological landscapes are represented on the drums by zonal areas or borders that relate to hunting, fishing and trapping narratives. Painted ideograms serve as personal, cognitive maps for each Noaidi's soul-journeying. Demonstrated through two distinct styles made either from birch or pine and spruce tree wood, the design and construction of the Noaidi runebommes varied considerably across the Sámi regions, as did the meanings of the images painted upon them, which in recent centuries have been generalised and homogenised. Drums from the central Sámi regions

Sámi offering and praying at a mound grave as depicted in Religious Ceremonies of the World *by Picart*

combine the two traditional methods of drum construction.

Irrespective of how the Sámi tripartite universe is depicted—whether layered vertically or in concentric format—it consists of an upper domain reserved for higher spirits, a middle realm of living beings and a lower realm (Sáivu,) perceived as an upside-down world full of ancestral spirits of the dead. These worlds are connected with an invisible cosmic pillar having the Sun as its centre, surrounded by higher spirits, people, animals and other symbols. The location of the figures in relation to each other indicate a cyclic view of life.

Northern Sámi create bowl-shaped drums from the knots and boles of tree roots, preferably pine or spruce. The runebomme membrane depicts the three worlds layered vertically rather than concentrically. *Sáivu* is the Sámi's paradisial realm where all beneficent and ancestral spirits reside after death. Sámi believe that animals, birds and frogs have a *máddu* (soul) of their own and that they reside in the Sáivu realm. Powerful Noaiddit bind these animal spirits to themselves as allies. The *noaideloddi* (sorcery bird) brought the Noaidi's helping spirits from *Sáivu* to assist in trapping luck in the hunt. In other words, the Noaidi are able to lead the animal souls in the hunt to capture.

The frame-drums of the South Sámi peoples were traditionally oval in shape. Around the "Earth" edge of the drum, various pictographic figures depict the purpose of each drum, which varies according to need. Spiritual realms are portrayed between the edge and the solar-centred surface of each drum. Placed centrally, the Sun *Beaivi* is represented by a rhombus shape. Rays extend from each of the four points, depicting the cardinal regions of the Heavens—North, South, East, West. On the Lule type and northern drum, Beaivi became a rounded Sun. Along the rays of the Sun—*Beaivvi lážžit*—reindeer wander as symbols of the solar divine. Other higher spirits may feature here in this central zone. Metal (silver and brass) and bone charms attached to the back of the drum add further power and noise.

Cultic offering sites called *Sieidi* were constructed of tree stumps and rocks. These were placed at liminal markers where the water meets land or sky and where the Noaidi and the spirits they consult are called to meet through the yoik. Boulders or tree-stumps were covered with fat and blood to establish a reciprocal, mutually beneficent relationship. Certain Sieidi were chosen for their natural formations that suggest human or animal features. Propitiation was necessary for successful hunting—bargains were struck with *Sieidi* spirits, in which the kill or catch was shared. Traditional sacrificial offerings of reindeer or bear secured the power needed for making spirit journeys. Many families in Lapland have or had their own private *Sieidi* to propitiate prosperity and protection.

Although drums were sacred objects, ordinary people who were not recognised as official Noaidi shamans could use them in a limited capacity for generic divination, protection or guidance. Family drums were often stored by the fireplace. Spirit communication was achieved via an indicator—*arpa*—that moved around the drum membrane as it was gently beaten. Indicators were usually made of bone in the shape of a ring, animal, bird, fish or triangular pointer. Elder bark, when chewed, yields a dye resembling blood. This dye is used to paint the pictograms onto the drum membrane. Sámi pictorial art is a sacred process assigned only to genuine Noaidi. Main images include the Sun and Moon, figures of fertility and hunting, elementals of thunder, sea and land as well as numerous animals, namely Bear, Wolf, Crane, Black-throated Loon, Salmon, Beaver and Reindeer.

Runebommen, a ritual drum of the Sámi shaman

Design is dependent upon location. Hunting myths involving wild animals and a variety of water birds are associated with different star constellations and spiritual beings that dwell in Sáivu. Stick-like pictographs mirror the sacred landscape of the Sámi homeland and runebomme designs represent their relationship with spirit. Treated very much as art in an increasingly secular world, rather than as vibrant expressions of cultural identity, it is unsurprising that Sámi people are opposed to outsiders attempting to interpret their customs and lore based on these images.

Although drums are objects which have been preserved in obscurity for hundreds of years, their images derive from a time when people thought very differently, making understanding them quite challenging. Drum construction and decoration is the preserve of Sámi ethnicity. It is reclaimed as a spiritual crafting known as *duodji*—the weaving of folkloric and ancestral customs of indigenous tradition created as a narrative or visual mnemonic.

It is vital to understand how the spirits are perceived in Sámi society. As animists, Sámi believe in the imbued spirit of all things, from rocks to trees, and from the living to the ancestral dead. These spirits are not polytheistic Gods as modern Neo-pagans would perceive them, but divine emanations inseparable from their hosts and free of anthropomorphic expression.

Sharing archaic roots with the shamanic based cultures of Siberia and Mongolia, the Noaidi are the traditional indigenous shamans of the Sámi peoples of Fennoscandia.

Many Sámi today remain reluctant to discuss or reveal information relating to the spirit animals painted onto the original 71 drums and which are being reproduced on new drums for use within the modern Sámi community. There are certain customs and taboos about keeping the relationships and contexts between Sámi persons and spiritual animals secret, that are not observed by those outside the Sámi community (or sometimes within it,) especially by those working within the tourist industry. A sacred reciprocity exists between the Sámi and the spirits of their ancestors, the land and of the elements, that might be jeopardised if certain taboos relating to secrecy are not observed. To share such knowledge might cause illness, misfortune or, in the worst case, death. For similar reasons, the Sámi are reluctant to speak of their understanding of past sacrificial practices, especially with persons from outside the culture. They are no more willing to reveal their sacred sites. This, too, is related to the superstitions surrounding the taboos of secrecy with outsiders.

Because of societal and political changes in modern-day Sámi communities, a new paradigm is arising in the study of Sámi shamanism and art. Amongst the mountains and fjords of the Tromsø municipality of northern Norway, the Sámi Festival of Isogaisa has been held annually since 2010 in the town of Lavangen. The popularity of this venue has witnessed the rise in the practice of shamanism amongst the indigenous Sámi of Norway since its recognition as an official religion in 2012. The Sámi Isogaisa cultural festival provides a platform for dramatic ritual, dance, drama and song through which the Sámi may rediscover and celebrate their identity as a people. As with many pre-Christian customs, once revived, they adopt additional layers of meaning and means of expression. Nothing returns to how it was—it cannot. But this is no reason to lament this, for no other culture is the same as it was five hundred years ago, either. Science, philosophy, politics and religion have changed humanity irrevocably.

Many sacred symbols are now widely used for marketing purposes within the tourist industry. However, because the explanations that accompany them are based on interpretations recorded by 17th and eighteenth century missionaries, they are not necessarily accurate. Motifs from original runebommes and prehistoric rock art are now depicted on the clothes and accessories that are sold at the festival. A popular symbol that now emblazons many a *luhkka*—a Sámi cloak with a hood—is the Sun *Beaivi*. Adhering to old Noaidi traditions, less progressive shamans withhold such demonstrative exhibitions of their magics and continue to decorate only their drums with these sacred symbols. Sámi identity—suppressed for hundreds of years—is enjoying a renaissance at the Isogaisa festival. Former taboos on the use of drums, sacred symbols and the *yoik* are lifted and a dialogue between the past and the present is made possible, completing the revivalist celebration of Sámi culture—a bittersweet note in a modern world. At the Isogaisa festival, people once again communicate with the animate world. Animals such as reindeer, which were once sacrificed to the *Sieidi* at communal events, have been replaced by blood bought from blood banks. Through art and dance, the spirit animals which are now available to all festival attendants continue to be significant. In the shifting tides of a world sliding towards globalisation of industry and secularisation of belief, they are acquiring new meanings pertinent to that world. Spirituality is now a lifestyle choice, yet one emblazoned as a badge of honour for a people denied it for too long.

—SHANI OATES

YEAR OF THE WOOD SNAKE
January 29, 2025–February 2026

OVER FOUR thousand years ago Buddha, the Jade Emperor, invited twelve animals to attend his birthday party. As a reward each creature would be gifted with a year. The animal's spirit would rule its year and the spirit would hide in the hearts of those born then. Horse galloped rapidly, rushing to claim its year. Snake hid inside Horse's hoof. Upon arriving at the party Snake leaped out and the startled Horse fell back. Snake then jumped ahead, arriving before Horse. Thus Snake became the sixth of the twelve animals Buddha rewarded with stewardship over a year upon creation of the Oriental zodiac. Five Elements (Fire, Water, Metal, Earth and Wood) distinguish the animals. Every sixty years the pattern of Element-animal pairs repeats. 2025 is the Green Wood Snake's Year. Snake has a flexible and inspirational nature. Setting realistic goals to work toward cherished dreams this year replaces the Dragon's flash and flamboyance with a mysterious charm and elegance. Wisdom and strategy are the focus. Snake sheds its skin and emerges reborn, appearing transformed. This year brings significant changes, exploration of new opportunities and the release of old habits and fixed ideas. Uncoil. Slither forward and work your serpentine magic. This is thought to be a good time to have a child. Those born in a Snake year are often gifted and talented. Fashionable dreamers, they are also charismatic and charitable.

Chinese New Year commences with the second New Moon after the Winter Solstice. It begins in late January to mid February.

More information on the Wood Dragon can be found on our website at
TheWitchesAlmanac.com/pages/almanac-extras

Years of the Dragon
1929, 1941, 1953, 1965, 1977, 1989, 2001, 2013, 2025

Illustration by Ogmios MacMerlin

Same Sized Eyes

WHEN THE SKY is overcast, the clouds extend from overhead to the horizon in all directions. If thick enough they diffuse the sunlight so that the whole sky is a monochrome gray-white color. If the clouds are kind and thin a bit, you might spot a bright patch among the gray-white expanse. If they thin a bit more, they might be kindly enough to resolve the bright patch into a bright disc. The right amount of clouds will act as a giant filter, allowing you to view the Sun without discomfort.

Your viewing may only last a few seconds. Inevitably, the clouds will thicken and blot out the Sun, or the opposite—clouds will disperse and the Sun will become too intense for viewing. In those few seconds between clouding and clearing, you might appreciate the bright disc of the Sun looking surprisingly like the full Moon.

Likewise, during a not-too-cloudy night the full Moon might break through enough to appear exactly like a cloud-dimmed Sun. Normally people assume the Sun to be brighter and constant and the Moon dimmer and variable, but these are relative terms. If you view the Moon during the night when the sky is clear, you'll see her brightness staying the same all night long. During an overcast day the Sun's brightness can swing back and forth from undetectable to blinding. In these cases, the light of "th' inconstant Moone" is not variable, while the light of the cloud-covered Sun is not constant. You might recall from memory the brightness of both appearing to be the same, although you'll never see them in the sky looking the same at the same time.

If the Moon and Sun only occasionally resemble each other in terms of brightness, they always resemble each other in terms of size. The characteristics of brightness and size of Earth's lesser and greater luminaries in the heavens have been noted for millennia and are encapsulated in myth. In ancient Egyptian times Horus kept one eye on Earth during the day and the other at night.

However, solar and lunar sizes are an illusion. If you summoned the Sun towards Earth until he was the same distance as the Moon, you would see him covering the whole of the sky.

Conversely, if you pushed the Moon from Earth so she was as far away as the Sun, you might see her glowing nearby him as a star. No matter where you placed them, their absolute diameters—meaning both at the same distance from Earth, no matter what that distance might be—would show the Sun being quite large and the Moon being quite small. Astrophysicists say the absolute diameter of the Sun is about 400 times than that of the Moon—it would take 400 Moons side by side to cover the width of the Sun!

From Earth you don't see the *absolute* diameters of Moon and Sun—you perceive their illusory *apparent* diameters. Apparent diameter doesn't require both bodies to be at the same distance. Relatively speaking, the Moon is very close to Earth and appears larger, while the Sun is very far from Earth and appears smaller. The Sun may be 400 times wider than the Moon but the Moon is about 400 times closer to Earth—the two variables of diameter and distance for each luminary very nearly balance. From Earth, Horus' eyes appear the same size.

The similarity of size has important and beautiful consequences. During a total solar eclipse, the Moon just covers the Sun. Cross-eyed Horus! For a few minutes those lucky few in the Moon's shadow experience full nighttime on Earth. Historically, this was not so. Before scientific understanding and rituals evolved to help humans cope with what they were seeing, those unlucky few witnessing the eclipse most likely ran in terror for their lives as they were being followed by the Moon's shadow.

Many have attributed the nearly equal apparent diameters of Moon and Sun as another proof of the intelligent design of the cosmos, put there by the deities for human edification and amazement. Even now, when there are scientific models that can explain what's happening, the wonder (or terror) of eclipses can never be diminished. A person standing on Earth perceives Sun and Moon as equally sized, but whatever created the Universe (if anything created it at all) certainly didn't order them to be forever fixed at a precise distance from Earth for human benefit!

You can verify this by witnessing a certain type of solar eclipse. Sometimes eclipse viewers are treated to a literal ring of fire in the sky. This happens because during the Moon's monthly orbit around Earth her distance isn't consistent. Sometimes she's a bit further, sometimes a bit closer. If she happens to be a bit further in her orbit at the time of eclipse, she appears that much smaller and doesn't completely cover the Sun so the eclipse isn't total. Instead, it's known as an annular (from the Latin word for "ring") eclipse. At other times, the Moon doesn't travel directly in front of the Sun and she only covers a chunk, resulting in a partial eclipse. Solar attributes then become lunar—the Sun might appear like a brightly glowing, fat crescent Moon.

Whatever type of solar eclipse—total, annular or partial—seeing one is a transcendent experience. Humans living now are fortunate to be able to witness them. Future descendants won't be so lucky.

One of the first (and continuing!) experiments Apollo 11 astronauts set up on the Moon in 1969 was a series of mirrors pointing back at Earth to measure the Moon's distance. From Earth, lasers were aimed at the mirrors and extremely accurate measurements were taken. It turns out the Moon is slowly moving away from Earth at a rate of about an inch and a half (3.82 centimeters) per year—since the experiments started, the Moon has receded about six and a half feet or about 2 meters. That may not sound like much over the course of an odd half-century but the recession

is relentless. As the Moon continues to recede, she will no longer cover the Sun during a total eclipse. In the future people will see only annular and partial eclipses, total eclipses becoming the stuff of myth. Unfortunately, as the apparent diameter of the Moon continues to shrink, seeing an annular or partial eclipse will become more and more difficult. Further into the future the Moon will appear so small that even these eclipses will not exist. Her passage in front of the Sun will seem more like a transit of Mercury or Venus where these planets appear as small dark spots slowly crossing the face of the Sun and are visible only through a telescope.

Those viewing such future occurrences may not even be human since this process of recession will take millions upon millions of years. In that far distant future, there may not be anything on Earth—human or otherwise—to appreciate the heavens. It works the other way as well. Millions upon millions of years ago, nothing human and probably nothing intelligent witnessed eclipses—and no eclipses were visible to witness!

Astrophysicists agree the Moon was far closer to Earth when both were quite young, filling the entire sky most of the time. Not only that, but she was cruising! Where today she circles Earth in a

staid twenty-seven and one third days, back then she did it wantonly in 10 *hours*. They theorize that the gravitational forces between Earth and Moon were so intense that as they orbited each other, both bodies violently contorted, expanding and contracting like giant rubber balls. It's unlikely that any kind of life similar to what currently exists on Earth could have evolved on the molten heaving surfaces, or having evolved to that point, survived that kind of massive and periodic environmental instability.

Astrophysicists use the term *transit* when a smaller body crosses in front of a larger body. The term for a larger body crossing and covering a smaller body is *occultation*. Of course, the terms larger and smaller refer to perception of apparent (and not absolute!) diameters from Earth's surface. What is seen as the larger body may be relatively close to Earth while what is seen as the smaller body may be relatively far from Earth. By absolute measures, the smaller-appearing body may be the larger, and the larger-appearing body the smaller, as is the case when a planet occludes a star.

Solar eclipses can be considered as a special case of occultation between the similarly-sized Moon and Sun. Millions of years ago what occurred shouldn't be considered eclipses as they are currently understood. Now the similarly-sized luminaries intersect fairly rarely but back then the huge Moon constantly occluded the comparatively tiny Sun. The appearance of the Sun in the sky would have been the exception, not the daily occurrence that happens now.

The Moon appeared so large she would have been synonymous with the sky. Had anyone been able to witness it, during the course of a normal day the Moon would extend nearly from horizon to horizon, with a little sliver of space between her and Earth. Rarely, the Sun might peek out within that sliver of space for a short while until he was once again occluded by the Moon. It would take multiple millions—if not billions—of years before the Moon moved far enough away from Earth so that the Sun could have a whole day in the sky to himself!

Even though the Sun might eventually rule the sky for weeks or months at a time, the Moon would have occluded him quite regularly during the course of a year. These occultations could have been seen from nearly anywhere on Earth, and they must have been astounding to witness—a Moon a few times her current diameter passing in front of the smaller Sun for hours. Now that she has visually shrunk to her present size, from any specific location on Earth you can only ever see a total solar eclipse on average once every 375 years. The longest and rarest total solar eclipse you can ever witness lasts only about seven and a half minutes!

Eons ago and eons hence eclipses did not and will not exist. Past and future, Horus' eyes are unequally sized. Humans are now living on Earth during the era of the sweet spot—several million years on either side of present time when Horus' eyes are the same size and eclipses can occur. As fortune and evolution would have it, humankind is here to appreciate and celebrate their beauty—and that is cause for wonder and gratitude that you are alive right now.

—STELLUX

The Real Mary Magdalene

WHO IS the real Mary Magdalene? Is she a penitent prostitute or a representation of the divine feminine? Her role has been discussed and debated by scholars and academics over the last two thousand years. There are many Marys mentioned throughout the Bible. In fact, the name Mary occurs in the Bible more than any other female name. Some historians have suggested that the names Mary, Maryan and Miriam could actually be titles given to priestesses, so that Mary Magdalene could be Mary the priestess of Magdala. The name Magdala is likely to have come from the Hebrew word *M'gdal* which means pillar or watchtower, the type that shepherds used to watch over their flocks or it could simply mean that she took the name from the village of Magdala, which is along the shore of the Sea of Galilee, where she is believed to have come from. There is a Mary of Bethany, too, and

it is not certain that they are the same person. Mary is mentioned in all four of the canonical gospels of Matthew, Mark, Luke and John, which tell roughly the same story of her life but from different perspectives and they were written many decades after the events they recall.

Mary was thought to have left Israel to go to Egypt around the age of eleven or twelve and she became a devotee of the Goddess Isis and trained as a temple priestess in a temple devoted to Isis. Mary was taught the secrets of sexual alchemy, sacred femininity and the death rites that were practised in the Egyptian temples at that time. This put her in good stead for her future role of the Kingmaker—anointing the King of the Jews. When her training was completed, she returned to Israel and it was there that she met Jesus. Mary was from a noble family of the tribe of Benjamin—a prestigious tribe—and was of independent means. She became one of the disciples of Jesus and along with a few other women, Mary provided some money to financially help Jesus in his work. This version of her story is at odds with the common narrative that Mary was a penitent prostitute—she had no need to sell her body for money. She was trained in the sexual, feminine arts and this was probably one of the reasons for that label of prostitute being given to her. Another reason was to discredit her closeness with Jesus and the companionship they shared. Interestingly, there is no mention of her being a prostitute in the New Testament—this is a more modern description and was possibly linked to the knowledge she had gained from her temple training in sacred sexuality or it could point to the patriarchal structure of the Church suppressing the role of a strong female. The defamation of her character originates from Pope Gregory I, who in 591 CE talked about Mary in a homily. He called her a sinful woman and mentions a story from the Gospel of Luke in which seven demons were cast out from her, using this as justification of his assertion that she was unclean. The pope said that these demons filled her with loathing, hatred and greed and that she was dirty. He also stated that this story was evidence that her anointing of Jesus and use of perfumed oils were seduction attempts because she had lusted after Jesus. This spread as gossip and become ingrained in people's thoughts of her because if the Pope had said it, surely it had to be true. This smearing of Mary's character nevertheless aligns with the darker side of her, the underworld aspect. She was portrayed as an outcast, unclean, a fallen woman, whereas in reality she had power—the power of a strong female—and so men were scared of this and reacted by suppressing her. From this power came love, as she has a large capacity to love and to spread love.

There are reasons to believe that Mary and Jesus were actually man and wife. The act of anointing could be part of a marriage ceremony as well as the act of making a king. Mary and Jesus touched in public, which was illegal under Judaic law at the time. Mary was said to have washed his feet with her hair—perhaps an act of love rather than one of repentance. They were both thought to be in their thirties and to remain single at that age in Israel in that period was unusual.

The Nag Hammadi Gospels were found in 1945 along the banks of the Nile and they paint a different picture of Mary than that in the Bible. In these Gospels Mary is described as a teacher, a natural leader, a strong female and a source of great wisdom. These scrolls give a truer picture of her importance and close relationship with Jesus and her treatment by the Disciples. One theory is that these writings had been deliberately hidden and omitted from biblical records by Emperor Constantine who set up the Council of Nicaea in an attempt to mislead the Roman Empire, hiding the story of Mary and Jesus' true relationship. Alternative theories include that the Nag Hammadi texts were possibly mass-produced grave goods commissioned and deposited by Greco-Egyptian citizens, a practice well documented in this region. Another theory is that the codices were hidden by a group of monks for safe keeping away from the approaching Roman authorities.

The Gospel of Mary Magdalene, though, was not found at Nag Hammadi. It was actually found earlier in Upper Egypt along the Nile River and was sold to a German academic, Dr. Carl Reinhardt, in Cairo in 1896. Written in Coptic by her students and the community around her rather than by Mary herself, it was not in a well-preserved condition and as a result was very fragmented, with the first six pages missing entirely. It describes Mary's struggles after the death of Jesus and her lack of acceptance by the group formed by the Apostle Peter, who resisted female leadership. Peter's dislike for her is apparent, but the other Apostles turned to Mary for reassurance and wanted to know the secrets shared with her by her *Rabbonni* (teacher) Jesus.

After the crucifixion of Jesus, Mary was said to have fled Israel with her sister Martha, her brother Lazarus who was raised from the dead by Jesus, Joseph of Arimathea and possibly also a servant girl named Sarah. They left very quickly in a boat with no rudder, oars or sails. Were they trying to protect a pregnant Mary or were they being persecuted by the authorities? They were a wealthy group as Mary had her own money and Joseph was financially well off—he owned the plot Jesus was buried in—so surely they could afford a decent boat. The fact they fled in such a shoddy boat can be interpreted as evidence of a very quick exit. The refugees were believed to have arrived in France at Marseilles in the Aux de Provence region. The group dispersed and Mary remained in Marseille along with Lazarus for a while. Here she spent her time spreading the teachings of Jesus before her death in a cave near St. Baume some thirty years later.

As well as being a Roman Catholic Saint, Mary Magdalene is a Goddess of divine femininity, sacred sexuality and wisdom. She represents the balance of feminine power to the divine masculine energy of Jesus, but she is independent of him, too. Mary is the true embodiment of wisdom, of knowledge beyond imagination. She is symbolic of perseverance, going through great challenges and surviving to become a stronger person, for example, witnessing the torture and death of her beloved and then fleeing her homeland as a refugee. The early Christianity that she was charged to spread by her teacher, her Rabboni Jesus, is very different than the misogynistic church of most of Christian history, but the feminine energy of compassion and love is returning. The Rose Line priestesses are awakening. The matriarchal wounds are being healed. The love of the Magdalene will bring back the balance, the duality, the energetic life force of love back to humanity.

—CLAIR PINGEL

Merry Meetings

*A candle in the window, a fire on the hearth,
a discourse over tea…*

KNOWN AS the Official Witch of Salem, Laurie Cabot is a pioneering figure in modern Witchcraft. With decades of devoted service to the Craft, she has authored numerous books and founded the Cabot Tradition of the Science of Witchcraft. Laurie has dedicated her life to teaching and passionately advocating for the acceptance of Witchcraft as a legitimate spiritual path. Join us as we delve into her fascinating journey, her views on Witchcraft today, and the wisdom she lovingly imparts to both seasoned practitioners and curious newcomers alike.

What inspired you to become a Witch?

Many of my childhood friends were Catholic. At times, I would accompany them to their afternoon catechism, as well as attend religious services. Their instruction included the notion of God and the forces of evil in the devil that oppose him. It was not a concept that I could embrace. Even at such that early age, I was sure that there wasn't a devil. I asked some of their ministers and what I took away was that God was good and the devil was evil. They didn't just believe this; they were convinced of it and that the only resolution to this problem was to wash away evil. This notion and its wrongness stuck with me through my childhood.

As a youngster, I experienced many magical happenings. I remember an evening that I was sitting on the back porch of our home. I was there by myself, looking at the Full Moon. As I sat there gazing into the night sky, I had a vision of two little boys on bicycles near train tracks near a trestle. I saw one of

the boys fall down the side of the trestle, his body getting covered by dirt that landslided onto to him. In that instant, I knew exactly where it was. It wasn't near our home in Anaheim at all.

I ran into the house and related the entire vision to my mother, emphasizing that the boy was suffering and needed help. Because of my agitation, my mother phoned the sheriff's office and convinced them to check out the story. They indeed did find and save the boy. My mother did not question my abilities—it was not an uncommon occurrence.

After a time of going to catechism classes with my friend, I began to question what I sometimes heard. For instance, it had been said in one such class that "you cannot suffer a Witch to live." This bothered me so much that when I arrived home, finding my mother home in the kitchen, I asked "why do we have to kill Witches?" My mother's immediate response was that we were not going to kill Witches. She furthered the conversation by relating that there were good Witches and bad Witches, just like there

Laurie Cabot. Photo by Jean Reuud.

were good Catholics and bad Catholics. She added that we did not believe that Witches embodied the evil embodied in the devil. She reminded me that we did not believe in the devil.

Can you share a bit about Felicity, your initiation and the Kent witches?

In time, we made our way to Boston and began looking for books about psychic happenings. We really could not find much—it wasn't a popular subject at the time. In fact, there was not much about Witchcraft, per se. So I started to talk to the librarian behind the counter. She introduced herself, Felicity, and asked if we were truly looking for books on Witchcraft? I told her that I was, she told me that she was a Witch. I thought my mother would faint on the spot. She turned her face away, the blood draining from her face leav-

ing her a pale white.

She said that they had some books on Witchcraft, as well as some on the Golden Dawn and others that I can't remember. She indicated that she could not remember what was there, as they were all old and many were stolen from the collection. Oh, she mentioned Madam Blavatsky and Theosophy. In fact, there were many about Theosophy. But all in all, there were not enough books.

It was after this bit that Felicity mentioned that she had a Coven and that she would help me if my mother would allow it. We all ended up at her house. I think it was on Beacon Street. It was so long ago, I am unsure, but I do believe that it was on Beacon Street. It was one of those homes built with stone. When we arrived her husband was in their library. I think she showed us into the dining room. There were two other women there. She indicated that they were members of her Coven and that they were there to study with her.

Of course you have to remember, I was only a child. What she taught me was not fancy or overly wrought. It was folksy kind of stuff. For instance she taught me how to raise the wind. For that we went out onto her balcony. She put a bunch of feathers in my hand. She said to call the wind and to then blow the feathers into the air. She also taught how to cast a Circle, which she did by using the sword.

So that is how I met Felicity. I went there only a few times, maybe two or three times. My mother did not want me to become a Witch. I don't remember why I stopped going there, I was learning a lot from her.

When did you open your first shop?

I opened my first shop in 1971. It was called the Witch Shoppe. It was a very simple little bit of a shop, first of all.

It's a long story. I won't go through all the "stuff," but I was living in the North End for a short short time before I moved to Salem. I didn't want to move to there, but I met a person in the North End. She had two children. She moved from Rhode Island, and she said, "why don't we move together? We can split the rent and move to the suburbs. So our children don't have to be in the city."

I didn't want to move to Salem. My friend knew that I was a Witch. I told her that

I didn't want to move there not knowing the vibe of there and I certainly didn't want to embarrass my friend. Well, she went looking for apartments, and she showed up with a rolled up piece of paper. She hesitated about sharing. It was a place in Salem that just was right. That's how I ended up in Salem.

Before this even occurred, when I was in the North End, I made a vow to the God and Goddess that I would wear my robes forever so that people could find a Witch. I thought to myself, now all the nuns have given up their habits and they wear dungarees and sweatshirts. If you wanted to find one of them, you couldn't. I thought nobody in our community was wearing traditional black robes and using black coloring marks on the body. My thought was, it takes all the colors to create black. In using black you absorb

al the colors of the planets and the universe into your body. If you wear white, it reflects and reflects light. But black draws in and helps you to become more psychic and more sensitive.

So I decided to make a vow and I did and have kept the vow. In addition to wearing my robes, I decided to wear a pentacle. At that time, pentacles were not openly worn. I had a friend who was learning to work with gold, he made a pentacle for me. I went about with my pentacle and my robes.

We were moved to Salem on Chestnut St. which to me is architecturally the most perfect street in America. It was a really nice three-story house, 18 Chestnut St.

My first encounter was outside of a post office as a young man was coming out. He looked at me, stopped dead in his tracks, looked at my pentacle and stared at me for a minute and then ran away. I guess he understood that I was a Witch. That was the first time someone recognized me as a Witch and responded in a strong way. It was funny, I got quite a laugh.

Did owning a store influence your approach to presenting Witchcraft to the community?

Yes, I tried to make quick progress in the beginning. Of course everyone was against it at first. Because, it was just supposed to be commercial because of the history of Salem. It wasn't supposed to be real. But Salem was a good place to make the public aware. But there was resistance in the community, many did not want a public face. The first parade we had, there were only about six of us, and we had an escort on either side. It was actually comprised of my first students.

So we're marching in the parade and they put a broom on the shoulders of the escorts rather than a gun. They were marching with a broom. And as we were walking along the path., the reception we received was good, in fact many who saw us said they were happy that we were there. It made a difference in my internal focus. We also caught the attention of the Salem news along with other not local reporters. The New York Times sent reporters here to cover me, one of whom was a sportswriter. He wanted to know if I had predictions for him, as if I knew.

What advice would you offer to someone curious about exploring Witchcraft to help them get started?

Read books on Witchcraft. In this day there are plenty to read, and they're well written. A good start is The Power of the Witch, *my first book and is good for the basics. Christopher Penczak has many as well.*

How do the principles of Witchcraft shape your everyday life?

Well first, you have to apply the principles on a daily basis. It has to be rote. It can't be wake and say "I should do this, I shouldn't do that." It has to be a way of life. It can't be separated from life. You have to wake up and decide what you want or what you are going to do. You have to be well read. Don't just read about Witchcraft. Read about magic and science. Read about culture. In other words, you need to know about the world a little more.

Things are connected in the world, from culture to culture, there's a lot of connec-

tion when it comes to magic. It comes through from many centuries. You need to know your past as much as is possible. Read about ancient times How can you judge if you don't know it? It just leaves you impaired, without knowledge. There is wisdom in continuous learning. Our little brains can't hold everything, keep the information flowing. As you get older, the information will disappear from your brain if you are not constantly feeding it. You need to do this not just for yourself, but also for your family and your country.

How do you envision Witchcraft contributing to discussions on spirituality in today's world?

Well, it depends on who you reach and reaching the audience to hear what we have to say is the issue. Like I said, the statistics show that there are many Witches but you never hear of them. It's not newsworthy.

ARTHUR EDWARD WAITE

Mystic, Poet, Creator of the Modern Tarot

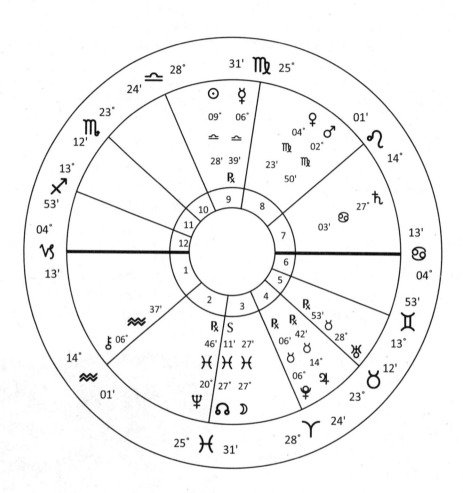

THE PACKAGING on the most familiar and popular of the numerous Tarot Decks available today is labeled with the names; Waite-Smith, Rider-Waite or Rider-Waite-Smith. Rider was the original publisher of the 1910 cards, Smith was Pamela Colman Smith, the artist who illustrated the 78 cards and Arthur Edward Waite was the British-American mystic, author and poet who conceived of the deck. His insight and vision in presenting today's Tarot cards has been the model for hundreds of different decks which have guided millions of aspirants and seekers for more than a century. His contribution continues to be significant today as the realm of esoteric study and mysticism expands in ever growing popularity.

Arthur Edward Waite was a Libra, born on October 2, 1857 at 1:00 pm LMT, in Brooklyn, New York. History tells that his parents were unmarried. In the nineteenth century that created major obstacles to pursuing opportunities. It clouded and blocked the social connections needed to assure a successful life. Some accounts state that the parents were married, but that his father died at sea and it was as a young widow that the mother returned to England. She took Arthur and his younger sister Fredericka along. Throughout his life the issue of illegitimacy haunted him, making him feel less than respectable. Pluto in his natal 4th house of parentage and heritage indicates a murky family situation and a missing parent. The family was not without funds, though for young Arthur was educated at a private school in London and later enrolled in St. Charles' College. His mother converted to Catholicism. This had a powerful impact on Waite's early spiritual development. Jupiter is in his 4th house. This placement often shows a very religious and rather well-to-do family background. In 1874 his sister died. That tragedy motivated Waite to seek answers through esoteric and spiritual studies. He began researching and studying at the British Museum Library. There he discovered the writings of Eliphas Levi and The Hermetic Order of the Golden Dawn. Waite joined the Order and also

became a Freemason. He was to spend most of his life in and near London writing for various publications. He edited a magazine, *The Unknown World*, which was dedicated to the world of metaphysics.

Looking at his birth chart, the Sun and Mercury conjunct in the 9th house support his international background and his interest in publishing, philosophy and scholarship. The Libra placements trine Chiron in Aquarius shows genuine ability and talent. He was highly thought of in the very active esoteric circles of his time. His important contributions touch on the entire metaphysical field. His Moon, North Node and Neptune are conjunct in Pisces, revealing profound intuitive ability and psychic gifts. Venus and Mars are conjunct in Virgo in the 8th house. Waite's grasp of creative detail

and interest in understanding the deep mysteries of death and the afterlife are also suggested by that strong 8th house Virgo emphasis. His first wife Ada Lakmen—whom he called Lucasta—died in 1924. This was another great loss to him following the deaths of his father and sister. He and Ada had one daughter, named Sybil. Waite married again in 1933 to Mary Broadbent Schofield.

He had Capricorn rising and Saturn in the 7th house. Biographical records describe Waite as rather rough, not a refined academic. He was inclined to degrade the efforts of fellow occultists. Pamela Colman Smith complained about how nominal the payment was for the now famous Tarot card illustrations he commissioned from her. There are also accounts of spiritual groups torn apart by internal feuding, which he was involved in. Uranus in the 5th house is sextile Saturn and also sextile the Pisces placements. This pattern indicates exceptional productivity, creativity and originality. Many of his writings remain in print today. These include *A Pictorial Key To The Tarot*, *The Holy Kabbalah*, *A New Encyclopedia of Freemasonry* and *The Book of Ceremonial Magic*. He also wrote two allegorical fantasy novels, *Prince Starbeam* and *The Quest of the Golden Stairs*. He wrote extensively about The Holy Grail and he edited an anthology of poetry and faery folklore titled *Elfin Music*."

In esoteric astrology the large number of retrograde planets in his natal chart would be interpreted to show that Waite was an old soul. He

THE EMPRESS.

expressed ancient wisdom he had gleaned in previous lives. Waite passed away on May 19, 1942 at the age of 84, near the time of his Uranus return. He is buried in Bishopsbourne Village, Kent, UK. Arthur Edward Waite's enduring contributions—in addition to the Tarot deck, have left a lasting legacy—benefitting present day occultists.

A. E. Waite Literary Insights

Arthur Edward Waite was a prolific writer and mystic. He is most remembered for his works on the Tarot as well as occultism and Ceremonial Magic. Here are some notable quotes from his writings:

1. *"The true Tarot is symbolism; it speaks no other language and offers no other signs."*

2. *"Behind the man is the Tree of Life, bearing twelve fruits, and the Tree of the Knowledge of Good and Evil is behind the woman; the serpent is twining round it."* (Key 6, The Lovers Tarot card)

3. *"All true religion, all true morality, all true mysticism have but one object, and that is to act on humanity, collective and individual, in such a manner that it shall correspond efficiently with the great law of development, and co-operate consciously therewith to achieve the end of development."*

4. *"Beneath the broad tides of human history there flow the stealthy undercurrents of the secret societies, which frequently determine in the depth the changes that take place upon the surface."*

These quotes reflect Waite's deep engagement with esoteric traditions and his belief in the symbolic power of the Tarot as a tool for understanding the mysteries of life. For more quotes and insights from Arthur Edward Waite, you might explore his seminal work, *The Pictorial Key to the Tarot.*

—DIKKI-JO MULLEN

Illustration from Belle and the Dragon. An elfin comedy *by Arthur Edward Waite.*

ARTHUR EDWARD WAITE
Born October 2, 1857
1:00 pm LMT
Brooklyn, New York

Data Table
Tropical Placidus Houses

Sun 9 Libra 28—9th house

Moon 27 Pisces 27—3rd house

Mercury 6 Libra 39—9th house (retrograde)

Venus 4 Virgo 23—8th- house

Mars 2 Virgo 50—8th house

Jupiter 14 Taurus 42—4th house (retrograde)

Saturn 27 Cancer 03—7th house

Uranus 28 Taurus 53—5th house (retrograde)

Neptune 20 Pisces 46—2nd house (retrograde)

Pluto 6 Taurus 06—4th house (retrograde)

Chiron 6 Aquarius 37—1st house (retrograde)

North Moon Node 27—Pisces 11—3rd house

Ascendant (rising sign) is 4 Capricorn 13

Life, Death and Runner Beans

IT MAY come as a surprise—an unwelcome one at that—to find an article on death in *The Witches' Almanac*. After all, every New Year is a time for optimism, beginnings and a renewed celebration of life. And while death is real enough, it is hardly a topic to dwell on. That would spoil any party!

The truth is, however, that almanacs have long acknowledged that each new beginning contains its own end. Nothing in life—not this life at least—lasts forever. For that reason, death and dying were seldom overlooked in these pages, both events implicit in the natural sequence through which all living things must pass. Indeed some almanacs (notably those with a religious bias) made a big thing of it, solemnly reminding readers of their mortality and urging repentance before the grave had a chance to reclaim them. Often, too, there were blank pages where family deaths as well as births and marriages might be recorded, with frequent reminders of the moral imperatives conducive to salvation. Not that such morbid concerns crowded out other, more worldly, topics, with plentiful advice also on how to secure the well-being of readers, of their households and—since these were often country folk—that of their crops and their livestock as well. One sample devotes two pages to cultivating runner beans.

In similar fashion Witchcraft is itself as much a celebration of death as of life. Long ago, solitary Witches intuitively discerned within nature the tangible expression of a wider, invisible reality to which everything around themselves essentially belonged, no less than humankind. They might not have heard of the Emerald Tablet—an occult work ascribed to Hermes Trismegistos and esteemed by Sir Isaac Newton, among others—but they privately acknowledged the fundamental unity of all things seen and unseen—an understanding which the Emerald Tablet's "as above, so below" message famously proclaimed. And that same correlation is still acknowledged—indeed celebrated—by contemporary Witches in their ritual practices whether private or within a group or coven. It is no accident that at every initiation the old self figuratively dies in order then to be reborn, outwardly the same but essentially different, given that thenceforth its every "now" is imbued with the forever.

Similarly, there is archaeological evidence that in prehistoric times, it was customary throughout the island of Britain to bury the dead on land that had once been home to the living. This reflected sacramentally—being as the bishop of Hippo would say its outward and visible sign—the existence of an Underworld to which human beings proceeded after death, which was home also to the Gods. Commonly referred to as *Annwn*—a variant of *Annwfn*—and implying great depth (*dwfn* being Welsh for "deep")—the name was bestowed also on its ruler. The Mabinogion suggest that its location lay beneath what today are the counties of Cardigan (Ceredigion) and Pembroke (Dyfed.) On the other hand, different sources place it under Harlech Castle in North Wales. The truth is, of course, that it is everywhere and nowhere.

Whatever its location, whether geographical or indeed even astronomical—for some placed it in the constellation known as Corona Borealis—the dead are assured of finding it. A common belief in Wales was that shortly before a person's demise, a candle which was invisible save for its blueish-white flame—"silvery" best describes its colour—would discreetly seek them out. Known in Welsh as *canwyll corff* or "corpse candle," it variously inspired dread, hope and tender reassurance. What everyone agreed was that by following its light, the dead eventually reached their destination, be it the Underworld just mentioned or the celestial Caer Sidi, home of the Goddess Ceridwen, an alternative proposed by the poet Taliesin. The latter was described as a spiraling or possibly revolving

This Neolithic dolmen (c.3,500 BCE) at Pentre Ifan, Pembrokesire was traditionally held to be one of the entrances to Annwn. The stones are from the same quarry, located nearby, as those used to build Sonehenge 140 miles distant. How they were transported from to their present location on Salisbury Plain is still debated by archaeologists,

palace and lay within a constellation which the astronomer Ptolemy would subsequently label Corona Borealis or Northern Crown.

Another widespread tradition, one that continued long after the Old Religion had been replaced (or rather usurped) by Christianity, was to place a red rose or even to plant a whole tree on the grave of anyone held in high regard by his or her kinsfolk, while a sprig of evergreen tossed into an open grave testified both to the decay of the body and the enduring aphysical existence of its sometime owner. Recourse was had also to vervain (*Verbena officinalis*,) which was not only a sacred herb said by Pliny the Elder to be particularly esteemed by the Druids but also one thought to offer protection against harm, notably the cunning wiles of ill-disposed warlocks and Witches.

In charge of our posthumous welfare, according to the same Welsh tradition,

Mari Lwyd (early Twentieth Century)

icance has been overlooked by folklorists. It involves the Mari Lwyd, a horse's skull, often with runic characters daubed on it. At the start of each New Year, this is paraded through villages either at the end of a pole or borne aloft by someone concealed by drapery beneath it, proceeding from cottage to cottage and pleading for entry. Householders had to outdo its quips and jests—often expressed in verse or song—in order to frustrate its ambitions and dispatch it on its way. Forgotten today, given the jollity attending its progress through each hamlet, is the *memento mori* it was intended to be, a reminder that in the midst of life, everyone—each individual—is in death. Forgotten also is that in the *Mabinogion* the horse, a white horse especially, is associated with the enchantress Rhiannon as well as with her son Pryderi. The two are compared more than once to a mare and her precious foal.

was Lleu (the Irish Lugh) or to give him his full name, Lleu Llaw Gyffes, who was the subject of a fanciful and magically eventful biography in the *Mabinogion*. Its text was compiled in the Twelfth Century but based on a far older oral tradition. Regarded by scholars and some modern Pagans as a solar deity, the name Lleu is derived from the Indo-European root *lewk* meaning light or brightness, which survives to this day in the Welsh words *lloer* and *lleuad* for Moon. The Welsh for Sun is *haul*, presumably a derivative of the Greek *Helios*.

From the Welsh Triads (*Triawd Ynys Prydein*) we learn that Lleu was the owner of a yellow-white horse—its name Melyngan Mangre means precisely that. The connection survives in another folk custom still prevalent in Wales—chiefly in the South—although its Pagan signif-

Happily, to occultists of every persuasion, death means change rather than finality. And while never welcome—to think otherwise would demean the privilege of life—it is not something to be dreaded, still less feared. Sooner or later the *canwyll corff* will seek out each and every person, while nobody can resist forever the sweet cajoling of the Mari Lwyd. Yes, those practicing the Craft and occultists generally know of a reality beyond the here-and-now, indeed may even have experienced it from time to time, but they know, too, that for now it is the here-and-now that matters.

After all, someone has to keep an eye on those runner beans.

—DAVID CONWAY

Gods of the Sky

For the ancients, the Elements and forces of wind and sky were often personified as deities. The Egyptians envisioned Hathor as a Sky Goddess in the form of a hawk and as Sky Goddess of the Milky Way. The ancient Mexican Aztec religion saw Quetzalcóatl, the Feathered Serpent, as the God of the Wind that Blows in the Rain, and the Finns envisioned the forest Goddess Annikki as Mistress of the Storm Winds.

Hathor, Hawk of the Sky

I built a house for the Goddess
made of the wood of the sycamore tree.
Under the leaves of the palm tree
I eat bread in honor of Her.

Hathor, hawk of the sky,
rest in the limbs of my tree.
Hathor, house of the sun,
live in my house forever.

—EGYPTIAN INSCRIPTIONS AND
BOOK OF THE DEAD

Hathor means "House of Horus," the "house" being her womb, making her the mother of Horus. She may also have been Horus' wife originally. A daughter of Ra, cow-headed Hathor had a number of titles. Evan Meehan of Mythopedia gives a list which includes, "the Primeval, the Lady of All, Lady of the West, Lady of the Holy Country, the Foremost One in the Barque of Millions, the Distant Goddess (a name she shares with Sekhmet and Bastet,) Hathor of the Sycamore, Lady of the Southern Sycamore, Hathor of the Sycamore in All Her Places, Hathor in All Her Places, Hathor Mistress of the Desert, Hathor Mistress of Heaven."

A supreme Mother Goddess, she is also associated with love and pleasure. The Greeks and Romans even saw her as an aspect of Aphrodite. She had a violent side, too, and in her rage she would transform into Sekhmet and attack those who were disrespectful of Ra. She would also appear in the guise of a serpent and attack followers of Set—everywhere Set's supporters' blood fell, it transformed into Juniper berries.

Hathor has been worshipped for five thousand years as the Primordial Goddess who created the world and the universe, making her self-created and her own mother, called both the Primeval and the Lady of All. Meehan relates another tale that while sitting under a sacred Sycamore tree, Hathor guides and feeds the dead with milk and nourishment from her seven cows, or refreshes them with pure water. However, the dead still have to work for their supper by plowing.

She is also the Goddess of the Milky Way, the river of milk that comes from her cow. As a Sky Goddess she is called Lady of Stars and Sovereign of Stars. The festival of her birth is the day of the rising of the star Sirius (Alpha Canis Majoris or the Dog Star, known as Sothis in ancient Egypt,) which is July 19 in the Julian calendar, an event that heralds the coming inundation of the Nile. As the Celestial Nurse she nursed the Pharaohs as a cow or as a sycamore fig (*Ficus sycomorus*, an ancient and sweet fig species that contains a milky white fluid and has medicinal properties.)

The Mother of Mothers, Hathor is a Goddess who presides over love, conception, fertility, women, children and labor. As the Seven Cows she predicts the fate of a child when it is born. As patroness of beauty and cosmetics she inspires those who love objects of beauty. As the Mistress of Turquoise and the Lady of Malachite she is the patroness of miners of turquoise, malachite, gold and copper. She is also the patroness of dancers and musicians and Jenny Hill of Ancient Egypt Online tells that her son Ihy is a God of music and dancing.

While often portrayed as a woman with cow horns and a solar disk, she may also be depicted as a lioness, a serpent, a sycamore tree, a papyrus plant (reed,) a goose, cat, lion, malachite or a sycamore fig. She is associated with the constellation Ursa Major and the Dog Star Sirius. Sistrums—musical instruments with transverse metal rods that rattle when they are shaken—were played at her rituals and wine and beer flowed. Offerings to her include mirrors, perfume, music, dancing and alcohol. She is especially fond of Myrrh incense.

Quetzalcóatl, God of the Wind that Blows in the Rain

Called Feathered Serpent, Plumed Serpent, Ehecatl-Quetzalcóatl (Wind,) Kukulcán, Q'uq'umatz, Topiltzin-Quetzalcoatl (One-Reed, a reference to the calendar day on which he was born,) Tlahuizcalpantecuhtli (Venus,) Xolotl (Dog Twin,) the Feathered serpent of ancient Mexican Aztec religion was a God of water and Earth who is also associated with the wind that blows in the rain. Mike Greenberg of Mythology Source

Hathor shown with cow ears fragment of the capital of a column

says that Quetzalcóatl was the God of the Morning and Evening Star (Venus) as Venus appears in the sky at the start of the rainy season, bringing green life back to the Earth, making him as well a God of fertility and vegetation.

For the Aztecs he was the patron deity of priests, calendars and books—which he invented—as well as of craftsmen and especially of goldsmiths. He was sometimes a God of both death and resurrection. He and his siblings were credited with being the creators of the cosmos and of fire and of humanity. Before the Aztec people had maize, he turned himself into a black ant and followed other ants over a mountain as they were journeying to the maize plants. He then brought back a seed for the people and they were able to transition from harvesting wild plants to planting cultivated crops.

Xolotl the God of Death was Quetzalcoatl's twin or other half, which is why he has both death and fertility associations. In some accounts he is the son of Ōmeteōtl, a binary God/Goddess pair—Ometecuhtli and Omecihuatl—who created the universe. Other legends say that he was the son of Mixcoatl the God of the Hunt and the Goddess Chimalma, whose name means Shield Hand. Mixcoatl once shot Chimalma with an arrow because he was angry that she had spurned him, but Chimalma caught the arrow with her hand, which is how she got her name. The pair later reconciled and married but were unable to conceive until Chimalma prayed to Quetzalcóatl and swallowed a gem, after which she became pregnant with Topiltzin-Quetzalcóatl.

The flying serpent Quetzalcóatl frequently fought against his brother Tezcatlipoca the black jaguar. Each of their four battles defined one epoch of history and the dawning fifth age coincided with the time that the Spanish appeared. According to Evan Meehan of Mythopedia, since no one knew what guise Quetzalcóatl might take when he returned, Emperor Moctezuma II had this in mind when he learned in 1519 that the Spanish had landed on the eastern coast. Was this the return of Topiltzin-Quetzalcóatl, who had departed to the East by sea? Was Hernán Cortés who arrived with mysterious winged ships the reincarnation of Quetzalcóatl? According to

Quetzalcoatl image, Pyramid of the temple of Quetzalcoatat

Spanish reports Moctezuma sent gifts of ceremonial vestments and food to the Spanish just in case Hernán Cortés was a deity, out of respect. But the conquistadores soon proved by their brutal actions that they were the furthest thing from divine beings.

According to legend, in his human incarnation Quetzalcóatl was once the priest-king of Tula, the capital of the Toltecs. He did not participate in human sacrifices, instead only offering serpents, birds and butterflies. Tezcatlipoca, deity of the night sky, used black magic to depose him, getting Quetzalcóatl so drunk that he slept with his celibate priestess sister. Ashamed at what he had done, Quetzalcóatl walked to the Atlantic Ocean and then set himself on fire, rising to become the planet Venus. In another story he sailed to the East on a raft made of snakes.

The expulsion by Tezcatlipoca may have been the memory of an actual historical event. The early Toltecs had a peaceful religion that was changed when warlike immigrants and a military ruling class took over.

Quetzalcóatl's temple at Tenochtitlán was round because it is easier for the wind to move freely around a circular building. In the same city, the world's largest pyramid was dedicated to him. Quetzalcóatl is depicted as a feathered serpent or as a bearded man. In his guise as Ehécatl the Wind God he wears a mask with two tubes through which he blows the winds and a conical hat. He may have a black body with red and green feathers around his body and carries flowers. He is sometimes shown with a conch shell symbolic of the wind and is accompanied by his namesake the *quetzal* bird. To the modern Pagan, he can be interpreted as embodying the serpent aspect which relates to the Earth and to wisdom, and the feathered aspect that relates to the winds, rain and sky.

Julia Flood of Mexicolore states that his favorite colors are blue and black or red and white pinstripe. In Book I of *Florentine Codex or General History of the Things in New Spain*, the sixteenth century Franciscan Friar Bernardino de Sahagún describes Quetzalcóatl as bearing wind-associated symbols on his shield, carrying an arched spear and wearing turquoise earrings, a gold shell necklace and rattling anklets. He had a quetzal bird and his face was covered in a layer of soot.

Offerings to him can include the burning of copal incense and anything involving wind such as a song, a flute melody or even breath. Fresh flowers—especially sunflowers—and tobacco would be suitable plant offerings. Mesoamerican foods such as tomatoes, chili, squashes, potatoes, pinto beans, avocados, vanilla, pineapples, prickly pear cactus, jicama, papaya, guava, chocolate and corn would be appropriate. The altar could be decorated with pottery or statues from the Aztec areas and a conch shell.

Annikki, Mistress of the Storm Winds

"*Fair and goodly maid, Annikki, Of the Night and Dawn, the daughter, Who awakes each morning early, Rises long before the daylight...*" –Kalevala, tr. John Crawford 1898

A Finnish forest Goddess, her mother Mielikki (from Old Finnish *mielu* "luck") is a Goddess of the hunt, forests, bears, healing, luck and abundance. Her father Tapio (from *tapiola*, Old Finnish for "forest,") is a God of the woods, the hunt and bears.

Annikki is mistress of wind magic, for example, in the Kalevala as translated by Crawford, when a sailor refused to tell her the truth about where he was going, she threatened him with the following spell: "*With the winds I'll fill thy vessel. To thy bark I'll send the storm-winds, And capsize thy ship of magic, Break in pieces its forecastle, If the truth thou dost not tell me. If thou dost not cease thy falsehoods, If thou dost not tell me truly, Whither sails thy magic vessel.*"

She is also mistress of herbs and of herbal magic. The following passage (also from Crawford's translation) describes what she did to prepare a magical bath for her brother to help him woo a maiden: "*Warmed it with the knots of fir-trees, That the thunder-winds had broken; Gathered pebbles from the fire-stream. Threw them in the heating waters; Broke the tassels from the birch-trees, Steeped the foliage in honey, Made a lye from milk and ashes, Made of these a strong decoction. Mixed it with the fat and marrow, Of the reindeer of the mountains, Made a soap of magic virtue, Thus to cleanse the iron-artist, Thus to beautify the suitor, Thus to make the hero worthy.*"

In modern tradition, sacred to Annikki are all kinds of wild game and berries. While her name originated as a diminutive form of Anna, by meaningful circumstance it holds further secrets—*anti* means gift or forest, and—*kki* means giver of berries. Make a gift to her of berries and drop them into the fire.

–ELLEN HOPMAN

The Longest Moonth

Thirty days hath September,
April, June and November.
All the rest have thirty-one,
excepting February alone,
which only has but twenty-eight days clear
and twenty-nine in each leap year.

YOU MAY remember some variant of the above ancient rhyme.

This version of *The Days of the Month* dates from around 1555. It and many others describe which months are how long while also helpfully reminding you to add a leap day to February— although this version doesn't say how often you should do this!

As most people learn when very young, with the exception of February all months are either thirty or thirty-one days. The thirty-one-day months or long months are January, March, May, July, August, October and December. The thirty-day months or short months alternate with them for the most part, again excepting February and, curiously, July and August which are back-to-back months of thirty-one days. The longest month doesn't appear to be any particular one, since seven of them contain thirty-one days.

You might consider then what you mean when you use the word "month."

The Latin word *mensura* means "measure" and has bequeathed English a variety of words embodying the concept of measuring. One very old geometry and trigonometry book from the 1700s is entitled *Mensuration* and discusses in detail the measuring and calculating degrees of angles and lengths of sides of triangles and other polygons. Although similar, the word "menstruation" measures something very different, the period of a woman's menstrual cycle. Both Moon and menstruation cycles occur over the course of about a month. Instead of the word menstrual, "menses" is a term sometimes used, which literally translates from Latin as a plural of the word for "month." The word itself thus expresses the tight conceptual interweaving of menstrual and Moon cycle lengths, as when women in polite society used to get their "monthly."

Certainly the Moon's cycle was one of humanity's earliest constructs to track a length of time longer than a day yet shorter than a year. The convenient length of a month became a standard unit of time measure and was handy for understanding the transition of seasons and when agricultural tasks needed to be done. Different cultures had different names for each full Moon which were used as a schedule for communal activities. "Harvest Moon" or "Salmon Moon," for example, were named to designate the times to conclude the harvest or to commence fishing. The Moon as seasonal marker, scheduler and timekeeper pervaded all cultures everywhere. In Old English the word

for the Moon was *mona* and by adding the -th suffix the word became a unit of measure for one lunar cycle, or a mona-th. Substituting another suffix, the Moon's special day in Old English became mona-dae, an honor to the Moon sadly lost upon modern people as Monday signifies the end of the weekend and the start of the dreaded workweek.

There are various types of months. Usually the word "month" implies the *solar* month—one of thirty or thirty-one days long, or twenty-eight days for February or twenty-nine days once in a while. In contrast, a lunar month is a unit of time measuring exactly twenty-eight days long. To differentiate it from a solar month, call it a "moonth," a derivation from the Old English mona-th. Now every good Witch knows a Moon cycle is twenty-nine and a half days long. However true, for the moment consider a moonth to mean only a lunar calendar month of twenty-eight days and not a Moon cycle of twenty-nine and a half.

In many ancient cultures, calendars were based on the lunar cycle and the appearance of the first bit of waxing crescent signified the beginning of the cycle and was acknowledged by ritual. Later cultures based their timekeeping on a lunisolar calendar. Still later cultures—most notably the Egyptians—established a strictly solar calendar for secular use but retained the old lunar calendar for religious activities as have Hebraic, Islamic, Indian and Asian cultures. Unfortunately, like in ancient Egypt, modern solar months do not sync with Moon cycles. You can see that by examining the icons for the Moon representing her phases that are scattered throughout a solar calendar's pages, if the calendar manufacturer bothers to include them at all!

You may have known that a human gestation is about 280 days, commonly accepted as a bit over nine months long (and you certainly do know that if you have ever carried a gestating human!) However, that's nine months when you're counting by solar months (you could call them sunths?)—those of thirty or thirty-one days. Or twenty-eight, or twenty-nine. As odd as February is within the solar calendar with its status of being the shortest of the short months, its count of twenty-eight days echoes earlier lunar calendar standards composed of moonths. Counting by lunar months, human gestation is exactly ten moonths. One pregnancy calculator from the 1970s was designed like a circular slide rule and actually had markings entitled "Lunar Months" (along with weeks) on the inner dial with the solar months marked on the outer dial. The inner dial had several markings, two of which were used to denote a certain moonth wherein a woman perceived the first fetal movements in her womb or "quickening," which occurs during the fourth lunar month or between the sixteenth and twentieth weeks. It also had markings for her to note her last period, her ovulation, her likely times of abortion and finally her "estimated date of confinement"—or when birth would likely occur at the fortieth week or tenth moonth mark. By sliding the last period marker to any solar date, a mother-to-be knew at a glance all the other critical dates of her pregnancy in terms of weeks, moonths and sunths!

Counting by moonths may simplify the estimation of critical pregnancy dates but a year composed of only lunar months wouldn't do as a calendar, which should also correlate with the solar cycle of 365 days. It falls short, as twelve months of twenty-eight days is only 336 days. But why should a lunar calendar be bound by the solar convention of a dozen months? Since you're using a lunar standard, make the lunar calendar consist of *thirteen* or a coven of *lunar* months. By adding those extra twenty-eight days to the calendar you end with 364—short of a standard solar year by one day. Much closer, but why should a lunar month be bound by only twenty-eight days? Why not also add an extra day? In fine February fashion, add that day to the thirteenth lunar month, making twenty-nine days, and you have a total of 365 days within a lunar year, aligning with the solar standard. Did the phrase "a year and a day" originally reference a lunar calendar of 364 + 1 days?

Using this new lunar calendar of months, you can simplify the old *Days of the Month* ditty and needn't worry about which month has how many days (excepting the thirteenth):

Days twenty and eight
hath every moonth,
A dozen times repeat.
Append a moonth with
one more day
And calendar's complete!

...or nearly so. Like the solar calendar, there is still the problem of "leap" once every four years. Just like the solar calendar, it's remedied by adding an extra day to any month during a leap year:

Yet count half of half a day
each year,

142

So in four years one whole,
Then tend such whole day
to a moonth
And leap hath reached its goal.

This version of *The Days of the Moonth* dates from around 2024.

As described earlier, as a unit of time measure a sunth or solar month may have a variable number of days. Specifically, there are four different versions of the length of a sunth ranging from twenty-eight to thirty-one days. The same applies to a moonth which up until now has had just two different length versions, twenty-eight or twenty-nine days. Since it is a definable unit of time measure, it needn't be restricted to just those twenty-eight or twenty-nine days. Since the Moon has several cycles, there can be several different lengths of moonth:

There's the tropical moonth of twenty-seven and a half days, which represents the time it takes for the Moon to return to the same celestial longitude, which is just the terrestrial longitude projected onto the dome of the sky.

There's the draconic moonth which is seven seconds longer than the tropical moonth, reflecting the time it takes the Moon to return to a lunar node. The nodes are the two points in the Moon's orbit where eclipses may occur, and in older cultures were considered the head and tail of a dragon, hence the name "draconic."

There's a sidereal moonth of twenty-seven and one-third days, which is the time it takes for the Moon to return to the same position in the sky. *Sideris* is the Latin word for "star," implying that the Moon had traveled one cycle and was now back where she started relative to the stars.

There's the anomalistic moonth, of twenty-seven and a half days, the time it takes the Moon to return to perigee or apogee, the point in her orbit when she is closest to or furthest from Earth.

There's the synodic moonth with which most Witches are familiar, of twenty-nine and a half days and otherwise known as a "lunation," which is the time it takes for the Moon to return to a given phase, say full Moon to full Moon. "Synodic" comes from Greek σύνοδος meaning "meeting."

By putting a list of sunths and moonths together, you have the following types of months of increasing length of time:

Month Type	Length in Days
Tropical Moonth	27 1/5
Draconic Moonth	27 1/5 + 7 sec.
Sidereal Moonth	27 1/3
Anomalistic Moonth	27 ½
February Sunth	28
Standard Moonth	28
Leap Sunth	29
Leap Moonth	29
Synodic Moonth	29 ½
Short Sunth	30
Long Sunth	31
Gestational Moonth	280

Instead of days you could also quantify gestation in terms of moonth in which case it would be ten and sunths in which case it would be nine and a quarter. Since you're using the Moon as the time measuring standard, why confine a moonth to just a count of days? What about a count of years?

143

As noted, an anomalistic moonth is twenty-seven and a half days long. The perigee and apogee that define the anomalistic moonth are not fixed points in space, however, and like the Moon these points slowly orbit Earth. Once every eight and four-fifths years the lunar perigee and apogee points are back where they started. These two points are known as the lunar apsides, so consider the length of time of their orbit to be an apsidal moonth.

The draconic moonth of twenty-seven and one-fifth days also has a somewhat similar cycle. The lunar nodes are also not fixed points in space but very slowly orbit the Earth in retrograde motion, meaning they move opposite to the way the Moon and lunar apsides do. It takes them eighteen and three-fifths years to return to where they started. These two points are known as the nodal apsides, so consider the length of time of their orbit as a nodal moonth. You can add these two to the list:

Month Type	Length in Years
Apsidal Moonth	8 4/5
Nodal Moonth	18 3/5

It appears, then, that the nodal month of eighteen and three-fifths years is in fact the longest month. But there's another lunar cycle to consider.

Before considering that, consider the following: if you were to count by seconds, it would take you ten seconds to count to ten. No big effort, you would think. To count to one hundred, it would take a bit longer, just about one and two-thirds minutes. No problem, you'd insist. You might even be willing to attempt to count to one thousand or ten thousand, but soon there would be a problem and a very large one at that, as you will soon see. Here's a listing of numbers and the length of time it would take to count to that number:

Number	Length of Time to Count
1	1 second
10	10 seconds
100	1 2/3 minutes
1,000	16 2/3 minutes
10,000	2 4/5 hours
100,000	27 4/5 hours
1,000,000	11 ½ days
10,000,000	1/3 year
100,000,000	3 years

Notice that by the time you count to a hundred thousand, it's taking you over a day, counting one at every second. To count to a million, it's taking you a week and a half. To count to a hundred million, it's taking you on the order of years and by the time you count to a billion, a few decades or about one third of a century will have passed. A billion is a very large number indeed!

Because astronomers and astrophysicists deal with very large quantities in their work, they define an "eon" of time as a measure of one billion years. And so by that measure, Earth—along with the rest of the solar system—is about four and a half eons old. The whole universe is about fourteen eons old. This solar system has existed for about one-third of the time the universe has.

This last lunar cycle happens extremely slowly, so much so that it has never completed once. Modern physics has acquired more evidence to suggest it won't ever complete, at least as originally proposed. The Moon was born or formed near Earth. As youthful daughters sometimes do, she moved away from her mother but at a rate far slower than a snail's pace. She continues to move away from Mother Earth even now, four and a half eons later. At some point she will have reached her maximum separation from Mother, perhaps at the end of her maidenhood. Then she will embark on motherhood herself, slowly starting her journey back towards Earth. When she is well into her crone years, she will reunite with her Mother. She will be so close that you would see her once again fill in the whole of the sky as she did when she was born. However, at this Second Coming the increasing gravitational force between Mother and Daughter will cause Earth and Moon to deform. Under the stress, being the less massive of the two, Daughter Moon will break

down. Earth will then join the club of large outer planets in this solar system possessing a ring around the planet. The Earth will bend the rubble of the Moon around her—Moon will be transformed into Earth rings. At least that was the theory decades ago of how this last lunar cycle would complete— born around Earth, the Moon moved out, will travel to a maximum distance, will turn around, will move back in, then will die around Earth.

Witches understand the allusion of maiden, mother and crone to reference the cyclical monthly Moon phases. They also understand it to define the eras of a woman's life and so the allusion is extended here for the whole lifespan of the Moon. In honor of the Greek Moon Goddess Cynthia, call the timespan from lunar birth to lunar death a "Cynthiation," and add the term to the list:

Month Type	Length in Eons
Cynthiation Moonth	50

This single cycle of lunar birth, movement away from Earth, movement towards Earth and eventual lunar

death was calculated to take fifty billion years, more than three times the current age of the universe. Since no one ever observed nor measured the whole of this cycle, its length of time was a theoretical instead of an actual value. Unfortunately, the theory responsible for the extreme length of time for this Cynthiation to occur assumes that Mother Earth and Daughter Moon are the only two objects in the universe.

That is not to be the case. The Sun exerts a strong gravitational force on both Moon and Earth and in time will impact both rather profoundly and not just through gravitation. The Sun—along with the rest of the solar system—is now about four and a half eons old. As astrophysicists learned more about stellar evolution, they realized that as the Sun ages he will transform from a mellow yellow star into a red giant (popularly understood as the Sun "going nova.") In so doing he will increase the amount of energy reaching Earth, to the point where the oceans will boil off and life as it currently exists will end. His diameter will expand and extend beyond the orbits of Mercury and Venus. Later, a second solar expansion will cross Earth's orbit and possibly the orbit of Mars. Like the rest of the inner solar system, both Mother Earth and Daughter Moon are fated to be incinerated by the Sun when they are both about ten eons old. With the understanding of the lifespan of stars like the Sun, it became clear that the theoretical Cynthiation cycle of fifty eons would never complete. However,

it will complete when the Sun goes nova and the Moon is destroyed when she is ten eons old. You can add and update those terms to the list:

Month Type	Length in Eons
Cynthiation Moonth (theoretical)	50
Cynthiation Moonth (predicted)	10

Measuring by the Moon may mean many lengths of time as the magnitude of a moonth may be defined as a count of days, years or eons. Although five and a half eons is an immense amount of time, it is still a *finite* amount of time. Earth approaches the end infinitesimally with every passing moonth, when far into the future the Cynthiation cycle completes.

—STELLUX

portal [pawr-tl, pohr-]

noun
1. a doorway, gate, or other entrance, especially a large and imposing one.
2. a website or web page providing access or links to other sites, e.g., "many healthcare providers already utilize portals through which a patient can access test results."

The Mystery and Mystique of Portals

THE DICTIONARY definition of portal somewhat hints at what mystical portals are. In recent years the meaning of the word portal has become skewed from the first definition. Seekers who would tread the path of the mystic while living the magical life see portals differently. In the spiritual sense a portal marks a different kind of gateway. In metaphysical circles portals define doorways or openings to states of higher consciousness, for example experiencing other times and places. Accessing these portals brings a rarefied life experience in a tangible and different realm.

An excellent famous example of crossing through such a portal and back again involved time travel. On August 10, 1901 two British ladies, Charlotte Anne Moberly and Eleanor Jourdain, were vacationing in Paris. They traveled by train about twelve miles from the city to visit the palace of Versailles. Little did they suspect that a supernatural experience on that simple day trip would define the rest of their lives. These two Edwardian ladies were both well educated and respectable. Charlotte was the daughter of the Archbishop of Salisbury and Eleanor was an academic, the principal of St. Hughes College in Oxford. On that warm summer afternoon while strolling through the palace they suddenly found themselves looking at Marie Antoinette, peacefully sketching in her garden. The day shifted to October 5, 1789, in what were probably the last happy moments of the Queen's life. An angry mob was gathering and about to descend. Charlotte and Eleanor felt that they were in the eighteenth century throughout that fateful day. Then just as quickly as they had entered the portal, they returned to the early twentieth century and the experience was a memory. The two tourists described the event and gained instant notoriety. Eventually they wrote a book about their experience, titled *The Adventure*. Their credibility was questioned and Eleanor was even forced to resign her position at Hughes College. Still, throughout the years that followed, the pair remained adamant that they really had visited another time.

Other examples of crossing portals are described in the popular *Outlander* books and films as well as in the Harry Potter series and the Chronicles of Narnia by C.S. Lewis. In the novel *A Connecticut Yankee in King Arthur's Court,* Mark Twain describes how an engineer from New England is transported from 1889 to King Arthur's Camelot.

Have you ever felt that time somehow disappeared at some point? Or perhaps you were driving and didn't know how you had arrived at a particular destination because you didn't recall the journey? Reports of aliens appearing and then vanishing, sightings of sasquatch, the Mothman, the Jersey Devil and other unfamiliar or intrusive visitors have also been linked

to beings traveling through energy portals. A film from 1938 has surfaced showing a woman strolling through a crowd holding a cell phone. Had she been photographed while visiting from another time?

In seeking to transcend the limits of everyday reality, some feel that being aware of certain times and visiting certain places can enhance the ability to move through a portal into another dimension. By all reports the experience is unexpected, sudden and brings a total immersion, then it ends just as immediately and completely. Groups will sometimes gather for meditation and ritual in order to attempt to access a portal. A sense of the surroundings seeming different prevails when that happens. Labyrinths and sacred sites such as stone circles and places of worship have been places where such energy shifts have been experienced. Scotland's Rosslyn Chapel—a Templar mausoleum for the Sinclair family, who are said to be descended from a Holy Bloodline—is a place

related to the opening of a portal. Author W. F. C. Wigston describes Rosslyn Chapel as "the cradle of Scotch Masonry, if not of something deeper still."

Sunrises and sunsets, those liminal times when day turns to night and vice versa, are also linked to the opening of portals. Solstices and Equinoxes, Candlemas, May Day, Lammas and Halloween are other powerful dates when sacred energies might activate a portal, as are New Moons and Full Moons, particularly when the lunations occur during eclipses. August eighth (8/8) marks the peak of an annual portal called the Lion's Gate, which is thought to open on July twenty-eighth and remain accessible through August eighth. The number eight suggests the cosmic lemniscate or infinity symbol and the angel number 8-8-8. Lion's Gate, observed annually on August 8th, symbolizes the convergence of cosmic forces, notably Sirius aligning with Earth and the Sun in Leo, offering a heightened period of awareness beyond conventional perception, with effects felt from July 26 to August 12, peaking on 8/8. Those who are attracted to the Lion's Gate claim it draws upon the Egyptian mysteries. It involves heightened vitality and enhanced spirituality. Astrology and Numerology combine in various ways, pointing to when a portal might be accessible. Another portal has been said to open on November eleventh, when the 11/11 brings in the influence of Scorpio combined with the master number eleven's vibration. January first—the 1/1 number of the New Year—as well as birthdays and important anniversaries mark other potential portal opening times.

—DIKKI-JO MULLEN

the fixed stars

Capella

Horn of Plenty, Glorious Crown

DEEP SPACE. That inconceivably vast stretch of the universe beyond our familiar solar system sparkles with countless multi-colored stars. Certain stars have long been noted by astrologers and are considered in interpreting astrology charts. This has been happening since star gazers first linked the patterns in the heavens to earthly destinies. The fixed stars highlight significant events and offer details contributing accuracy and depth to astrological forecasts. The term "fixed" is something of a misnomer. The stars do move, but very, very slowly— barely a degree in a century.

Each year *The Witches' Almanac* features a different star. Capella is this year's selection. Called the Patron Star

of Babylon, Capella is the sixth brightest light in the night sky. It appears as a single star but is actually a quadruple star system 42.9 light years from Earth. Capella is a luminous bright yellow and is of the same spectral class as our Sun. When observed low in the sky it sometimes flashes red and green. The name comes from the Latin word Capa for female goat. Capella (also called Alpha Aurigae) translates to Little She-Goat.

This dualistic but mostly benevolent star is linked to the goat who nurtured baby Zeus. Playfully, the divine baby broke off one of the goat's horns. Zeus (Jupiter) placed the broken horn in the heavens to become the Cornucopia, the Horn of Plenty. It has also been called Glorious Crown. Its influence radiates a solar quality. Ptolemy related Capella to a Mercury–Mars energy while Alvidas noted a Mercury–Moon influence. Ambition, controversy, envy, dissipation, curiosity, honor and exploration of mysteries—both mundane and mystical) are traits that have been attributed to Capella. Currently it is at 22 degrees 11 minutes Gemini. An image which illustrates Capella is "A Man Playing Musical Instruments." The conjunction is the only aspect considered with interpreting the influences of fixed stars. Capella's impact when conjunct the luminaries and planets

Capella's impact when conjunct the luminaries and planets

Those born between June 10th and June 15th of any year will have Capella conjunct the natal Sun. Versatility, quick speech, wealth and vacillation are some relevant characteristics.

Conjunct with the Moon quarrelsome, domestic disharmony, many journeys

Conjunct with Mercury, success after great difficulty

Conjunct with Venus writing ability, popularity, honors

Conjunct with Mars annoying manners, wasted time and effort on trivialities

Conjunct with Jupiter intellectual curiosity, pursues legal matters, ecclesiastical connections, much travel

Conjunct with Saturn shrewd, tidy, upsets in relationships

Conjunct with Uranus eccentric, inventive

Conjunct with Neptune courageous, ambitious, issues with poor health. During the coming year a Jupiter transit will conjoin Capella from April 23–May 17, 2025. Venus will conjoin Capella July 22–26, 2025.

—DIKKI-JO MULLEN

Moon Cycles

A New Moon rises with the Sun,
Her waxing half at midday shows,
The Full Moon climbs at sunset hour,
And waning half the midnight knows.

NEW	2026	FULL	NEW	2027	FULL
		Jan 3	Jan 7		Jan 22
Jan 18		Feb 1	Feb 6		Feb 20
Feb 17		Mar 3	Mar 8		Mar 22
Mar 18		Apr 1	Apr 6		Apr 20
Apr 17		May 1	May 6		May 20
May 16		May 31**	June 4		June 18
June 14		June 29	July 3		July 18
July 14		July 29	Aug 2		Aug 17
Aug 12		Aug 28	Aug 31*		Sept 15
Sept 10		Sept 26	Sept 29		Oct 15
Oct 10		Oct 26	Oct 29		Nov 13
Nov 9		Nov 24	Nov 27		Dec 13
Dec 8		Dec 23	Dec 27		

*A rare second New Moon in a single month is called a "Black Moon."
**A rare second Full Moon in a single month is called a "Blue Moon."

Life takes on added dimension when you match your activities to the waxing and waning of the Moon. Observe the sequence of her phases to learn the wisdom of constant change within complete certainty.

Dates are for Eastern Standard and Daylight Time.

presage

by Dikki-Jo Mullen

ARIES, 2025–PISCES, 2026

"NOW is the true Age of Aquarius," astrologers the world over are saying.

"When will things return to normal?" many ask.

Never. A new normal is emerging to create a very different world. Hold on for the ride! Ancient prophecies about this time in history are coming true daily. This year marks the passing of the first quarter of the first century in the new millennium. Pluto—the cosmic transformer related to endings and beginnings—has completely crossed the cusp, leaving Capricorn behind to begin a 20 year passage through Aquarius. This shift last took place in 1777–1797. It marked the gateway to many changes in society back then, such as the rise of democracy, transportation methods, communication, science and much more. This current Pluto in Aquarius cycle holds amazing possibilities. Space travel, artificial intelligence, world governments and economic values may be the focus. During 2025–2026

Neptune and Saturn will both enter Aries. Fiery new concepts applying to spiritual quests and an overall pioneering spirit regarding security needs indicate the creation of a new frontier. The Aries eclipse on March 29, 2025 unveils specifics. Virgo and Pisces eclipses in September, 2025 and in February and March, 2026 indicate trends regarding healthcare, ecology and empathy for the unfortunate. Uranus—hovering on the Taurus-Gemini cusp—relates to extreme weather and Earth changes.

For personal insights, start with the forecast for your Sun sign. It's the familiar birth sign everyone knows. Next consider the forecast for your Moon sign. Your Moon addresses the personality, emotional needs and instinctual responses. Finally, turn to the forecast for your rising sign, the Ascendant. This segment relates to your physical presence and appearance in the world around you. Learn about all of this and more

ASTROLOGICAL KEYS

Signs of the Zodiac
Channels of Expression

ARIES: fiery, pioneering, competitive
TAURUS: earthy, stable, practical
GEMINI: dual, lively, versatile
CANCER: protective, traditional
LEO: dramatic, flamboyant, warm
VIRGO: conscientious, analytical
LIBRA: refined, fair, sociable
SCORPIO: intense, secretive, ambitious
SAGITTARIUS: friendly, expansive
CAPRICORN: cautious, materialistic
AQUARIUS: inquisitive, unpredictable
PISCES: responsive, dependent, fanciful

Elements
FIRE: Aries, Leo, Sagittarius
EARTH: Taurus, Virgo, Capricorn
AIR: Gemini, Libra, Aquarius
WATER: Cancer, Scorpio, Pisces

Qualities

CARDINAL	FIXED	MUTABLE
Aries	Taurus	Gemini
Cancer	Leo	Virgo
Libra	Scorpio	Sagittarius
Capricorn	Aquarius	Pisces

CARDINAL signs mark the beginning of each new season — active.
FIXED signs represent the season at its height — steadfast.
MUTABLE signs herald a change of season — variable.

Celestial Bodies
Generating Energy of the Cosmos

Sun: birth sign, ego, identity
Moon: emotions, memories, personality
Mercury: communication, intellect, skills
Venus: love, pleasures, the fine arts
Mars: energy, challenges, sports
Jupiter: expansion, religion, happiness
Saturn: responsibility, maturity, realities
Uranus: originality, science, progress
Neptune: dreams, illusions, inspiration
Pluto: rebirth, renewal, resources

Glossary of Aspects

Conjunction: two planets within the same sign or less than 10 degrees apart, favorable or unfavorable according to the nature of the planets.

Sextile: a pleasant, harmonious aspect occurring when two planets are two signs or 60 degrees apart.

Square: a major negative effect resulting when planets are three signs from one another or 90 degrees apart.

Trine: planets four signs or 120 degrees apart, forming a positive and favorable influence.

Quincunx: planets are 150 degrees or about 5 signs apart. The hand of fate is at work and unique challenges can develop. Sometimes a karmic situation emerges.

Opposition: a six-sign or 180° separation of planets generating positive or negative forces depending on the planets involved.

The Houses — *Twelve Areas of Life*

1st house: appearance, image, identity
2nd house: money, possessions, tools
3rd house: communications, siblings
4th house: family, domesticity, security
5th house: romance, creativity, children
6th house: daily routine, service, health
7th house: marriage, partnerships, union
8th house: passion, death, rebirth, soul
9th house: travel, philosophy, education
10th house: fame, achievement, mastery
11th house: goals, friends, high hopes
12th house: sacrifice, solitude, privacy

Eclipses

Elements of surprise, odd weather patterns, change and growth are linked to eclipses. Those with a birthday within three days of an eclipse can expect some shifts in the status quo. There will be five eclipses this year—two are total and three are partial.

March 29, 2025—New Moon—partial solar eclipse in Aries, North Node

September 7, 2025—Full Moon—total lunar eclipse in Pisces, North Node

September 21, 2025—New Moon—partial solar eclipse in Virgo, South Node

February 17, 2026—New Moon—partial solar eclipse in Aquarius, North Node

March 3, 2026—Full Moon— total lunar eclipse in Virgo, South Node

A total eclipse is more influential than a partial. The eclipses conjunct the Moon's North Node are thought to be more favorable than those conjunct the South Node.

Retrograde Planetary Motion

Retrogrades promise a change of pace, different paths and perspectives.

Mercury Retrograde

Impacts technology, travel and communication. Those who have been out of touch return. Revise, review and tread familiar paths. Affected: Gemini and Virgo

March 15–April 7, 2025
in Aries and Pisces

July 18–August 11, 2025
in Leo

November 9–29, 2025
in Sagittarius and Scorpio

February 26–March 21, 2026
in Pisces.

Venus Retrograde

Venus retrograde influences art, finances, and love. Affected: Taurus and Libra

March 2–April 13, 2025
in Aries and Pisces.

Jupiter Retrograde

Large animals, speculation, education, and religion are impacted. Affected: Sagittarius and Pisces

November 11, 2025–March 11, 2026
in Cancer.

Mars Retrograde

The military, sports, and heavy industry are impacted. Affected: Aries and Scorpio. There will not be a Mars retrograde this year.

Saturn Retrograde

Elderly people, the disadvantaged, employment and natural resources are linked to Saturn. Affected: Capricorn and Aquarius

July 13–November 28 2025
in Aries and Pisces.

Uranus Retrograde

Inventions, science, electronics, revolutionaries and extreme weather relate to Uranus retrograde. Affected: Aquarius

September 6, 2025–February 4, 2026
in Gemini and Taurus.

Neptune Retrograde

Water, aquatic creatures, chemicals, spiritual forces and psychic phenomena are impacted by this retrograde. Affected: Pisces

July 3, 2025–December 11, 2025
in Aries and Pisces.

Pluto Retrograde

Ecology, espionage, birth and death rates, nuclear power and mysteries relate to Pluto retrograde. Affected: Scorpio and Aries

May 5, 2025–October 14, 2025
in Aquarius.

ARIES
March 20–April 19
Spring 2025–Spring 2026 for those
born under the sign of the Ram

Aries, the Ram—the first of the zodiac signs, is associated with the Vernal Equinox and is always about freshness and new beginnings. A cardinal Fire sign ruled by feisty Mars, Aries dwells in the present and prefers to get to the point with things. Impulsive and assertive, you are the competitive and courageous pioneer who approaches each day as an adventure.

The Springtime begins with both Mercury and Venus retrograde in Aries. An impromptu reunion with longtime friends would be enjoyable. Late March favors completing projects. Expect life to turn in a new and different direction after the solar eclipse on March 29. Mars affects home and family dynamics during the first half of April. Attend to home repairs and maintenance. Make time to help a relative who is facing a challenge. April 16–May 9 is a productive cycle for both study and travel. On May Eve dedicate a ritual to acquiring needed information and making wise choices. Late May through June 5 allows business and pleasure to combine gracefully. A considerate coworker becomes a supportive friend. Mid to late June welcomes a refreshing energy which highlights leisure time interests. Sports and games are likely to be involved. Near Midsummers Day a goal is within reach.

Throughout July until August 6 Mars affects your health sector. Strive to release stress. A steady, gradual approach is best regarding daily work and exercise. Don't over do it. At Lammas sip a tisane of fresh peppermint with a meal featuring whole grain bread and seasonal fruits. Late August–September emphasizes teamwork and equality. A relationship is challenging. A commitment can reach a turning point. At the Autumnal Equinox meditate on justice. The Full Moon in Aries on October 6 brings perspective and corrects an imbalance. From October 14–November 6 a Venus influence brings success and recognition to someone who is close to you. Sharing in the celebration of another's achievement will cement an important bond. Halloween plans can involve recognizing an important milestone.

Early November–December 13 brings an energy surge. An upbeat Mars aspect inspires you to move forward in pursuit of a dream. By the Winter Solstice an answer to a query or application arrives, bringing needed information. A journey brings a reward at Yuletide. You can especially enjoy viewing Winter scenery and unusual holiday decorations in late December. As January begins several planetary transits affect your career sector. You may feel anxious about relationships with colleagues and wonder how others might impact your own opportunities. The week of the New Moon on January 18 favors making adjustments and strengthening alliances. Late January ushers in a cycle of stronger support from others.

Becoming more active in an organization can be worthwhile. At Candlemas light a white candle and offer a toast to honor an acquaintance whom you admire. A request you make will be met with a favor being granted.

During February an influence from retrograde Jupiter can tempt you to risk a gamble. Postpone taking a chance with high stakes until after March 11 if you feel any qualms. It's tempting to go to extremes. A Venus influence during the last part of February supports charitable endeavors. Volunteering to help either people or animals who are in need can be very rewarding from February 10–28. Reflect upon ways you can give back to the community. What you have to offer? Time management and the wisdom of experience will be themes in your life starting on February 13 when Saturn crosses the Aries-Pisces cusp for the final time. Winter's final days promise insights concerning the results of your past efforts and choices. The mood softens a bit when Venus enters your sign on March 6. A caring friend or relative offers a helping hand. You will feel loved and appreciated. Share a humorous anecdote or enjoy a craft project to lighten a burdensome situation during the last days of Winter.

HEALTH

Healthwise Aries relates especially to the head, including the eyes and brain. Saturn, which always impacts health, will enter Aries this year. It would be a good idea to have a routine eye exam. Protect the eyes with sunglasses or safety lenses as needed. Wear appropriate head gear if encountering inclement weather or in any hazardous conditions. There can be some bouts of depression, especially near May 25 and July 12, 2025 or February 13, 2026. Focus on positive affirmations and maintaining good mental health during those times.

LOVE

Romantic attractions will often begin and end suddenly for those born under this fiery birth sign. Aries will usually welcome a challenge. April 18–June 16 indicates several promising influences for love involving the transits of Venus and Mars, the planets of affection and desire. August 26–September 18 and December 1–22 are excellent times to circulate and accept invitations. The stage for a promising love connection can be set then.

SPIRITUALITY

Neptune, a powerful indicator of spirituality, will enter Aries this year for the first time since 1875. Profound spiritual insights can present themselves before the end of March, 2026. This can involve completely new spiritual modalities or belief systems. Meditations involving colors can be instrumental in your spiritual growth this year.

FINANCE

Erratic and unpredictable Uranus will begin to exit your financial sector this year. The roller coaster ride which has affected your money situation for the past seven years or so is finally about to slow down. March 19–June 8 brings a favorable Jupiter trend. Explore promising earning opportunities at that time.

TAURUS

April 20–May 20

Spring 2025–Spring 2026 for those
born under the sign of the Bull

Taurus, The Bull, is a fixed sign of
Earth ruled by Venus. Sensual, stable,
calm and practical, you are the zodiac's
loyal builder. Comfortably anchored to
Mother Earth, creature comforts, quality, music and nature are likely to be
important priorities and focal points in
your life. You are a steadfast creature of
habit and usually will embrace a pre-
dictable schedule.

Recollections, reverie and remi-
niscences are your keynotes as the
Springtime begins because Venus is
retrograde until April 13. You will seek
peace and privacy then. A change of
pace develops from late April through
June 16 when a powerful Mars influence moves in. This encourages you
to make needed changes in your home
life and living arrangements. There
can be a family issue to address near
your birthday. June 1–8 the financial
situation brightens. Follow through
with an opportunity to add to your
income. Near the Summer Solstice
your energy level improves and you
are motivated to work on a cherished
project. Throughout July until August 6
the mood becomes light and playful. You
can be drawn to various games and other
leisure time activities. Make plans for a

late Summer vacation near Lammas.
Late August favors exploring options
and exchanging ideas. A relative or
neighbor offers insights and workable suggestions.

September's eclipse pattern affects
your social circle. A longtime friend
or coworker could consider a move.
Your support and approval can bring
needed encouragement regarding this
situation. At the Autumnal Equinox
a favorable Earth sign emphasis can
attract you to gardening or camping.
Enjoy the Autumn colors and revel in
the seasonal shift. During October an
opposition from Mercury sets off a
debate or controversy. Be diplomatic
and look at both sides if an issue is dis-
puted. A compromise might be the best
way to resolve things in order to assure
a happy Halloween. An opportunity to
travel to a sacred or haunted site arises
in late October or early November. The
Full Moon on November 5 reveals the
specifics. During the last three weeks
of November events pique your curiosity. You will feel the urge to unravel a
mystery. Answers come after Mercury
turns direct on November 29.

December accents the holiday traditions of other lands. Seasonal decorations and Yuletide foods and drinks with
an international flair will be appealing.
You might travel to a holiday market
or craft fair to purchase unique gifts. A
grandparent or grandchild participates in
a holiday event near the Winter Solstice
and invites you to attend. January 1–17
brings learning opportunities. Visit a
library or book store to examine new publications which are displayed. Enrolling
in a class or attending a lecture opens

new vistas of thought and changes a previously held belief. The New Moon on January 18 relates to errands and shopping. It's a good time to order supplies and browse catalogs and websites seeking worthwhile bargains.

The end of January combines social connections with a career goal. Befriend a colleague and discuss work concerns over steaming cups of tea or coffee. An unexpected and valuable bit of guidance is shared.

In February Uranus changes direction. New wardrobe items or an updated hair style appeals to you. A shift in the way others perceive you is developing. You will cherish an out of character yearning for a change in the status quo during February. More freedom and independence becomes a priority. At Candlemas light a single brightly colored taper to express individuality. From February 15–28 there is a competitive undertone. Maintain a sense of humor and select comic Valentine cards to offset subtle tensions with others. The eclipse on March 3 brings insight into the needs of a close friend or neighbor. Probe to find the root of what seems to be the issue. You have the opportunity to be a true friend. Avoid large crowds and gatherings during the last three weeks of March. You will seek quiet, peaceful times alone as Winter wanes. Privacy will be very healing.

HEALTH

The health of the throat and ears is often of concern to Taureans. Avoid prolonged exposure to loud noises. Wear a warm, comfortable neck scarf for protection from chills on wet, cold days. Uranus has been transiting your birth sign for the past several years, creating stress and an unsettled feeling which hasn't been the best for your health. Fortunately this situation will be drawing to a close this year. Your health should improve.

LOVE

Stability and commitment are important to this fixed, earthy, Venus ruled sign. Taurus tends to hold on when it comes to relationships and must be careful not to be overly possessive. June 6–July 2 and September 19–October 13 are especially promising for love connections this year. Play music or attend the opera or concerts to enhance your love connections.

SPIRITUALITY

The eclipses on September 7, 2025 and February 17, 2026 are times which favor gathering with like minded companions for group meditation sessions or discussions related to spirituality. Visiting a park, garden or forest to sense spiritual nuances emitted by the Earth will also uplift your spirituality.

FINANCE

A comfortable lifestyle enhanced by financial security is especially important to you. You never skimp on the quality of possessions, but you will shop for the best value regarding purchases. From June 10 throughout the Winter, Jupiter aspects your birth sign favorably. Your efforts to budget and manage money will be rewarded. The year's financial picture looks promising. Cultivate income producing opportunities.

GEMINI

May 21 – June 20

Spring 2025–Spring 2026 for those
born under the sign of the Twins

This mutable Air sign is ruled by Mercury. You are all about duality, the acquisition of knowledge and seeking a variety of experiences. Restless, intellectual, curious and sometimes scattered, the versatile sign of the Twins often combines several personalities in one. Your life is multifaceted. A pervasive nervous energy characterizes the alert and observant Gemini. Quick and eloquent, you excel at communication and are a natural teacher and storyteller.

Springtime arrives, bringing notes of reflection and nostalgia. Mercury is retrograde until April 7. Early April favors completing old business. A successful reunion or anniversary celebration can be planned near the Vernal Equinox. Unexpectedly you might run into an old friend on All Fools' Day. The 2nd and 3rd weeks of April emphasize financial gain. Pursue earning opportunities then. From April 18–June 16 a favorable Mars influence brings a burst of enthusiasm and energy. Much can be accomplished near May Day. Your writing and speaking abilities impress and motivate others. Share a joke or write a poem on May Day. Near the Summer Solstice a favor is returned making you feel cherished and appreciated. The month of July promises won-derful social opportunities. The entire month also favors creativity and artistic development.

Celebrate Lammastide as August begins by contemplating your long range goals. The steps to follow in order to manifest your dreams are revealed. Written affirmations can serve as a catalyst to facilitate concrete materialization. The eclipse on September 7 generates a surprising situation linked to your career path. Flexibility on your part helps to pave the path to success as the Autumnal Equinox nears. Late September through mid October brings time to pursue leisure time activities. Perfect your skills in playing a favorite game or your expertise at another enjoyable pastime. Late October through November 3 accents rapport with animal companions. At Halloween an animal theme costume would be a great choice. How about designing a black cat or a bat costume? Early November favors development of a more efficient and productive daily schedule.

From mid November through December 14, others will involve you in their plans and choices. Your cooperation and acceptance of this will make everything unfold smoothly. Let go and flow with the suggestions offered. A dynamic individual can seem a bit pushy, but is well intentioned and probably has good ideas to implement. The Gemini Full Moon on December 4 reveals the final outcome of a situation. There is an intriguing mystery to solve near Yuletide. Research would be helpful in solving a puzzle or enigma. On the longest of nights, the Winter Solstice, light bayberry and gold candles to attract prosperity and insight.

An awareness of afterlife connections and spirit guides intensifies near New Years' Eve. January 1–14 brings a return on an old investment or returns a forgotten dream. The last half of January generates a yearning to travel to new locations and explore unfamiliar subjects. Consider enrolling in a class or joining a tour group. February promises renewed inspiration and sparks enthusiasm for pursuing new options. On February 2, Candlemas, light five tapers in a rainbow of multi colors. Meditate in the candlelight for guidance regarding all of the possibilities which are available. February 26–March 20 brings a pervasive nervous energy. Don't try to multitask. Prioritize the projects which are already on your agenda. Gather any supplies or resources needed in advance to facilitate smooth going. The eclipse on March 3 ushers in a merry-go-round like flurry of activity. Life will be hectic but interesting. Verify times and appointments to keep the daily schedule organized during March. Winter's last days bring a sense of dejavu punctuated by memories. Observe and notice patterns in your life during March. The patterns will contain clues regarding the outcomes of important events.

HEALTH

March 19–June 9, Jupiter—the most benevolent of celestial influences—will transit Gemini, conjoining your Sun. This promises renewed health and vitality. Near your birthday health goals can be reached. March through June is a great time to start a fitness regime and to plan healthy meals. On July 7 Uranus will begin to enter Gemini. This Uranus trend is unsettling and will be influential during the next seven years. The development of a greater sensitivity to temperature extremes is one way this can link to your health. Cope by dressing in layered clothing to adapt comfortably to hotter or cooler surroundings as needed. Focus on controlling and releasing stress.

LOVE

Boredom often poses a threat to the long term associations in your life. Keep love connections interesting and alive by sharing travel or other enjoyable and stimulating activities with the one you care for. July, October and January 17–February 9 are three favorable times regarding love.

SPIRITUALITY

Past life studies can bring opportunities to deepen spirituality this year. Try a past life regression near the eclipse on March 29. The Nordic myths and mysteries hold spiritual truths which you can relate to. Purchase runes at Yuletide and work with them through the Winter days and evenings to awaken spiritual perceptions.

FINANCE

There can be some added expenses related to your home or workplace during both two week eclipse seasons of September 7–21, 2025 and February 17–March 3, 2026. Jupiter blesses your money sector from early July through February. Financial stability gradually builds near the pairs of eclipses. You can overcome any debts you might have accumulated. Those are also good times to form a foundation to address future financial needs.

CANCER
June 21–July 22
Spring 2025–Spring 2026 for those born under the sign of the Crab

The Crab, symbol of this Moon ruled cardinal Water sign, shelters a tender and vulnerable body inside its hard and crusty protective shell. Similarly, those born under this birth sign can appear outwardly gruff while guarding the tender emotions dwelling beneath. Coming from the primordial Water, Cancer reflects ancestral origins, empathy and memories. Sensitive and often introverted, this birth sign connects easily with those of a generation older or younger. Collectibles and collections can bring you pleasure, and possibly turn into valuable investments eventually.

The Vernal Equinox arrives with a dynamic Mars transit through Cancer. The pace is active and competitive through April 18. Your motivation is high. Much can be accomplished regarding your most important goals. Social connections are supportive during the last half of the month. Business and pleasure combine well during April. May brings a focus on time management. Include a date book and vintage time piece on your May Day altar to bless your time. Time, that most valuable, ephemeral and precious of assets.

Early June ushers in a strong financial focus. Efforts to add to earnings will be rewarded with profits by the 17th. As the Summer Solstice approaches plan an outing. You will feel restless and have a vague urge to travel, yet you might not have a destination in mind. The New Moon in Cancer of June 25 brings more specifics to light. A strong Jupiter influence during July intensifies the longing to explore new ideas and new places. Your birthday highlights adventure. By August 1 Venus enters Cancer. Assembling artistic seasonal decorations and a hosting a party following a Lammas ritual would delight friends and strengthen worthwhile social connections. Both love and money situations are auspicious early in August. Near the end of the month a complicated domestic situation arises. A home repair or the needs of a relative could require attention. Eclipses on September 7 and 21 stimulate a need to communicate and encourage a quest for information. A neighbor could seek support for a community project. Attend a neighborhood meeting and stay informed. At the Autumnal Equinox share seasonal stories and poems. Celebrate the Fall. Late September through October 14 an eloquence touches your words. Others are impressed by your ideas and may adopt your viewpoint. The last half of October through All Hallows' Eve is festive. Attend an art exhibit, concert or theatrical production with someone you care for. Love prospects are promising. Wear a romantic historic costume to Halloween themed parties and rituals.

November 1–18 brings a Mercury influence which directs conversations and thoughts toward health care. Publications and videos about maintaining wellness can be informative and helpful. The love and devotion of companion animals brightens your life during late November and December. A new familiar appears between December 12–22. Yuletide favors making a decision about an animal adoption. As you observe the Winter Solstice honor both domestic and wild animals. January 3 brings a Full Wolf Moon in Cancer which deepens heartfelt connections to creatures of all kinds. The first three weeks of January bring suggestions and ideas which present opposing viewpoints. Keep an open mind and get all sides of the story before making an important choice or decision. The week of the New Moon on January 18 accents teamwork and justice.

Financial management and budgeting become the focus as February begins. At Candlemas light green and gold candles to attract prosperity. February 3–March 2 favors delving into puzzles and mysteries. Helpful insights are uncovered. A whisper of guidance from the spirit world can clarify an issue. March 3–20 emphasizes travel and transportation needs. You will be out and about, keeping busy by juggling errands and appointments.

HEALTH
Wellness,of both the mind and body, are enhanced when the Crab is able to spend time near the waterfront. Walk in the waves, collect sea shells from the ocean's edge or take a boat ride. Allow the beautiful waters to wash away any tension, ills and ailments. Jupiter, the celestial healer, transits Cancer from mid June throughout the Winter season. This entire timespan is favorable for resolving health issues.

LOVE
Memories or regrets concerning a lost love can drift into your thoughts during the early weeks of Springtime. These are likely to be illusions, though— mere reflections of a situation which just wasn't meant to be. Push the sad thoughts aside and focus on the future instead. Venus points to promising love prospects during August and November. Circulate, accept invitations or plan a social event at those times to set the stage for true love to blossom.

SPIRITUALITY
The eclipses on September 7 and February 17 both carry profound spiritual implications for you. Explore new spiritual connections, studies or visit places related to sacred energies at those times. Dream interpretation can be helpful in understanding specific spiritual messages. It is always worthwhile for you to become familiar with the spiritual beliefs and practices of your ancestors. Hereditary factors as well as family heirlooms and keepsakes can play significant roles in your spiritual growth.

FINANCE
Kindly and thoughtful Cancerians can often be overly generous in gifting. This includes donating to charities as well as giving to friends and relatives. Always give only what you can comfortably spare and remember that offering encouragement, advice or time might actually help those in need more than offering money or expensive gifts would. With Jupiter transiting your Sun sign most of this year the overall financial situation should be bright. Real estate transactions and investments can be particularly profitable for you.

LEO
July 23–August 22
Spring 2025–Spring 2026 for those
born under the sign of the Lion

Leo, the Lion, is a fixed Fire sign ruled by the Sun. Charismatic and magnanimous as molten gold, you approach life with a dramatic flair. There is a royal touch in all you do. Proud and generous, you seek quality in everything and are reluctant to settle for less than the best. Others notice you as one who projects a warm, strong and dignified presence. Leisure and recreation, sports and gaming arenas will often have a link to your life purpose.

The gourmet within you surfaces during the earliest days of spring. Imported items, especially the fine foods and drinks of other lands, will appeal to you. March 30–April 14 draws your attention toward financial situations a spouse or partner has created. You will be very aware of how your status and destiny are intertwined with a partner's needs and priorities. By the end of the month progress is made with catching up on meeting financial obligations. A powerful Mars transit in Leo is in affect from late April until June 16. Your energy level will be high during this entire time. You will exemplify the saying "work hard and play hard." Others are impressed by your initiative and drive. May Day brings an exuberant feeling, try arranging a maypole dance or another bit of pageantry to honor the sunny spring days and season of flowers. May 13–25 is a time to be diplomatic. Expressing all you think in no uncertain terms could upset someone who sees your sincerity as bravado. Club and group activities can be fulfilling and productive near the Summer Solstice. You'll take pleasure in being one of the crowd.

Mercury makes a long passage through your birth sign, including a retrograde cycle spanning July, August and early September. You'll long to travel. A visit with friends and family can be rewarding. Renew long time connections. Near your birthday messages and suggestions arrive which can involve traveling to a destination wedding or vacation site.

During September be careful not to overextend financially by making a risky monetary move September 7–21. October finds you considering home improvements. Also a relative might surprise you with an invitation. A Halloween party for all ages could be planned for Halloween week. Choose a costume which features a clown or other humorous figure. Traditional games such as apple bopping or a jack o' lantern carving contest would be enjoyable suggestions for the party event. So would story telling and poetry readings featuring ghosts and the mystique of the season.

November emphasizes charitable endeavors and fundraising activities. You will feel the urge to make gestures of goodwill benefitting those less fortunate. Watch for omens related to angels which will assure you that your kind efforts are being noticed. The week of the New Moon on November 20 is a significant time to watch for benevolent signs of approval from the Spirit World to surface. During December a Venus transit adds a cheerful glow to the Winter holiday scene. Social prospects will be promising near the Winter Solstice Celebrate the shortest of days by spending some time outdoors. Winter sports or merely viewing the seasonal evergreens and Winter skies can be delightful. Travel is especially productive and uplifting December 22–January 1.

January brings a grouping of planets, including Mars, in your health sector. Others will want to talk about their well being. Listen—the conversations can bring worthwhile ideas regarding fitness. You'll feel quite proactive and enthusiastic as January begins regarding the quest to improve your own health. Consider joining a gym, a bowling league or hiking club. January 17–February 7 finds you praising the accomplishments of someone close to you. You will be proud of a partner or family member. At the Candlemas Full Moon in Leo on February 1 dedicate a pure white candle as an expression of gratitude for a special relationship. The remainder of February brings stimulating people into your work environment. A competitive colleague can inspire you to make a special effort with an assignment. Maintain an expression of goodwill and camaraderie and all will be well. Throughout March retrograde Mercury draws recollections of childhood experiences as well as past life memories to mind. Processing these ideas can enhance your self understanding.

HEALTH

The health of the back and spine can often concern Leos. Yoga sessions which address posture and relaxation can be beneficial. Making your fitness programs into social events—sharing the time with friends—will add to your dedication to maintaining wellbeing. Leo rules the heart. Keeping heart healthy foods such as fresh fruits and vegetables on your regular menu along with regular cardiovascular exercise will enhance your overall wellness.

LOVE

Respect is an important component in your love connections. You will cherish a love interest whom you can be proud of. Favorable love cycles this year span late August to mid September and December 1–23. The week of the Full Moon in Leo on February 1, 2026 promises revelations and insights, bringing an important love interest to light.

SPIRITUALITY

With the Sun as your astrological ruler the solar festivals associated with the solstices and equinoxes are meaningful times for heightening spirituality. Meditations and rituals connected to sunsets and sunrises often facilitate spiritual experiences.

FINANCE

The eclipse pattern this year has profound implications concerning your finances. Be aware of changing dynamics in current financial trends. A new strategy regarding money management might be worth considering. A Jupiter influence in the Springtime from March 20–June 9 indicates some promising financial opportunities developing then.

VIRGO

August 23–September 22

Spring 2025–Spring 2026 for those
born under the sign of the Virgin

Ruled by Mercury, Virgo, a mutable Earth sign, values practical knowledge and meaningful communication. Purity and precision are suggested by your symbol, the Virgin. Often portrayed holding a stalk of corn or wheat, she harvests health and service. Observant and analytical, Virgo is a natural troubleshooter and problem solver. Fulfillment comes through dedication. High standards are upheld, giving this birth sign the reputation of being a perfectionist and superior craftsman.

Patience is important as the Springtime begins, Mercury is retrograde until April 7. This brings old business to address. The last three weeks of April promise helpful suggestions and outreach from others. An offer or opportunity arises by May Day. May 2–June 9 brings new developments in your career field. Think of moving onward—go with the flow—to ensure success. A favorable Venus trend develops throughout the rest of June, bringing excellent social prospects. Accept invitations, especially if travel is involved. At the Summer Solstice include seasonal art and music in a ritual observance.

Mars transits Virgo throughout July and early August. Your energy and enthusiasm will be high, enabling you to accom-plish much. Don't give in to anger though. Employ humor and tolerance to dissolve a dispute near Lammas. Your thoughts will focus on club or group activities August 6–24. September is hectic and productive. Travel plans, perhaps to attend a conference, will materialize near your birthday. At the Autumnal Equinox business and pleasure harmonize. Express appreciation and gratitude with an offering of Autumn fruits and flowers. October 1–22 the financial picture brightens. Shop for items you've wanted—there are bargains to be found. Neighborhood activities set the pace near Halloween. Participate by serving hot cider and pumpkin treats.

November accents home life. You'll be inspired to redecorate and catch up on home maintenance. Visitors arrive unexpectedly November 10-30. Be tolerant and good humored if the conversation becomes controversial. Diffuse tension by encouraging others to speak. Early December brings happiness regarding the accomplishments of a close friend or relative. December 2–23 brings a focus on your heritage and family history. Share vintage photos and prepare a family recipe to serve on the Winter Solstice. The longest of nights brings a dream fragment about your childhood.

January 1–16 deepens a romantic connection. A giddy and youthful mood prevails. The remainder of January emphasizes your health sector. You'll be tempted to make some belated New Year's resolutions about wellness. A fitness program and healthy dietary choices may appeal to you as you look ahead at the times to come. Loving animal companions brighten the cold, dark days near January 25. A new dog, cat, horse or rabbit might become a part of your life then. This creature might be a powerful familiar.

At Candlemas light a blue taper to honor simple pleasures and peaceful days. February presents a new cycle regarding a group or team. A person who has been a fixture in your life becomes more interesting and unpredictable. Familiar faces move on and different ones appear. Near the eclipse on February 17 the specific details about this trend will become clearer. February 20–28 a unique sensitivity to and appreciation for sound and color is building within you. Try doing a craft project or attending a musical event to explore this dimension. The Full Moon in Virgo on March 3 is a total lunar eclipse. You will sense completion of past patterns nearing. Don't struggle against this. Adapting to what is trending and changing is wise. A Mars opposition to your Sun highlights Winter's final days. Others can challenge and inspire you. Thoughtful and cooperative responses on your part can put a positive twist on volatile situations.

HEALTH
Saturn, a health indicator, will transit your sector of partnerships during most of this year. Working on health issues with those closest to you will be important. The eclipses on September 7 and February 17 are likely to mark turning points in the well being of those who are close to you. Alternative health care and seeking second opinions from healthcare professionals can be valuable for selecting the best health care options this year.

Stress control and overcoming anxiety are important steps in maintaining optimum health. Take special care to relax and cope with sources of tension during July.

LOVE
Offering helpful criticism to loved ones to make them as perfect as possible often plays a part in the way you express true love. Soften any negative comments by tossing in a few compliments to remind one who is dear to you that they are cherished. September 19 through mid October and late December to January 16 are especially promising regarding love connections.

SPIRITUALITY
Neptune, which has a bearing on spirituality, is making a rare sign change this year. It will enter your sector of afterlife connections and secrets. This favors the development of mediumistic gifts. You may find, starting on March 30, that you are able to sense angels and other spiritual presences. Past life memories can intensify, heightening your awareness of spiritual connections. This awareness is likely to strengthen over the next 14 years. The Full Moon on October 6 begins a time when spiritual awakening is likely.

FINANCE
Your approach to financial management is usually analytical and will follow conventional guidelines. Many Virgos will begin to plan for retirement early. This year, beginning on June 10, a favorable Jupiter transit will enter your sector of goals, dreams and wishes. This is very fortunate for reaching financial goals. It remains in effect throughout the rest of the year.

LIBRA
September 23–October 23
Spring 2025–Spring 2026 for those
born under the sign of the Scales

Balance, art, harmony and fairness are the ideals which inspire and highlight this Venus ruled cardinal Air sign. Symbolized by the Scales of Justice, Libra promotes wisdom and righteous choices. Refined behavior, the quest for peace and diplomatic compromise will mark your interactions with others. Partnerships are especially important to Libra. You find truth and meaning through companionship. You seldom choose a solitary path.

A strong emphasis on the cardinal signs impacts Spring's earliest days. There is an impatient mood, bringing urgency. You will want to get things going immediately. The solar eclipse on March 29 clarifies this yearning through the choices and words coming from those closest to you. The first half of April brings a competitive situation to the forefront. Get others talking and listen carefully in order to fully understand this. May Day favors honoring those who have passed away. Plant a tree or assemble a floral bouquet as a memorial tribute. Throughout May and early June plans and wishes for the future will be a focus. You will overcome your characteristic indecision and vacillation and will feel inspired to concentrate on specific goals. June 9–26 business travel or messages connected to your work can

be important. At the Summer Solstice dedicate a crystal as a charm for clear communication and transportation. July emphasizes charitable endeavors. You might collect food or clothing to deliver to those in need or spearhead a fundraiser to support a worthy cause.

Near Lammas expect a "blast from the past." Early August renews a connection with someone who was in your life long ago. Good or not, history repeats itself at a rendezvous. August 7–September 21 Mars transits Libra. Your energy and vitality are renewed—life is busy and active. Look for constructive solutions to any conflicts which arise as the Summer ends. The Autumnal Equinox finds your curiosity piqued. Researching an interesting topic at the library or seeking expert advice to learn something new can be worthwhile September 23–October 5. Mid October through early November favors both financial gains and romantic interludes. A thoughtful gesture or invitation from a special someone brightens your birthday week. Your artistic talent is expressed near Halloween. You can assemble exceptional decorations or costumes. Include vintage or costume jewels and sparkles to add the perfect finishing touches to your creations.

November 10–30 brings a nostalgic and sentimental mood. Scrapbooking and adding to a cherished collection can be satisfying. Expect some activity in your neighborhood, too, with residents moving in or out. December brings a flurry of messages and invitations. You will be very busy early in the month. By the time the Winter Solstice arrives you will prefer to enjoy peaceful, quiet times at home.

Focus on domestic needs and family life December 21–31.

Neptune changes signs in January. This brings sensitive and mysterious people into your circle. A talented acquaintance can be a source of inspiration. At Candlemas dedicate a pale violet candle to truth and insight regarding a perplexing relationship. Someone might not be quite the person that you think he or she is. February 1–9 accents your love and pleasure sector. Hours spent socializing or pursuing sports, a favorite game or hobby is time well spent during February. The eclipse on February 17 accents health factors in your environment and also the wellbeing of others. Be aware of how people and places impact your vitality. Back away from whatever drains your energy or seems otherwise uncomfortable and risky. In March Jupiter changes direction in your sector of home, heritage and family life. A change of residence or a real estate transaction can be considered. New information about your ancestry might surface. Embracing your roots can be a helpful step in understanding yourself and your relatives. Winter's last days usher in a restless mood. Make an effort to concentrate on important priorities. Use valuable time, resources and energy wisely.

HEALTH

The eclipse on February 17 accents health factors in your environment. Be aware of how people and places impact your vitality. Back away from whatever drains your energy or seems otherwise uncomfortable and risky. Dreams frequently can bring valuable messages about your health. Try keeping a dream journal and interpret the symbols for insight into what your spirit guides are trying to tell you about maintaining wellness. Your lower back and kidneys can be vulnerable parts of the body.

LOVE

During the first weeks of Spring, before April 13, it's advisable to preserve the status quo regarding love. Venus will be retrograde then, so an impulsive break up or involvement could lead to regret. October and January are promising times for deepening a love connection. Share favorite desserts after a candlelight dinner or read a romantic poem to woo your loved one then.

SPIRITUALITY

July 7–November 7 Uranus will tickle the cusp of Gemini. That whole time period electrifies spiritual awakening. Try visiting a new spiritual group or meditation circle to discover new spiritual connections. Weather changes, especially lightning storms and wind, can carry spiritual messages. Research how various deities connect to wild weather. Call upon the Gods when the weather conditions are dynamic.

FINANCE

From the Vernal Equinox until June 8 a fortunate Jupiter influence favors your finances. Use this time period to prepare a budget and plan your financial strategy for the year ahead. Prosperity affirmations and visualizations can be especially effective this year. Consider pursuing financial opportunities abroad or which are otherwise connected to travel. Investments related to the fine arts can be lucrative for you.

SCORPIO
October 24–November 21
Spring 2025–Spring 2026 for those
born under the sign of the Scorpion

Ruled by Pluto this fixed sign of Water always delves beneath the surface. Identifying all that is distorted, broken and wounded, you are determined to find and fix that which isn't right. Intense, often suspicious, you can seem deep and mysterious. You scoff at the superficial. Strong passions and extreme emotions propel you through life. The Scorpion scrutinizes all and is seldom indifferent to anything or anyone. Keeping secrets comes naturally to you. You are always intrigued by puzzles and mysteries.

An upbeat Mars influence is present from the Vernal Equinox until April 16. The early weeks of Spring promise heightened energy and enthusiasm leading to accomplishment. April 17–30 social connections are stimulating and intriguing. The talent and creative efforts of a helpful acquaintance assist you. On May Day seasonal music and decorations set the pace for a productive month. Efficiency and organization make the time pass at a quick and satisfying pace during May. Others feel able to depend upon you. You will win esteem and loyalty. During June you can be drawn to academics. A trend begins which encourages widening your intellectual perspectives. There is so much

to learn. At the Summer Solstice consult books and other resources to understand the historic and mystical significance of the longest of days.

July 4–30 brings a sense of adventure. You would enjoy connecting with other cultures. Travel overseas or just visiting ethnic restaurants and import shops close to home can satisfy this urge to seek new perspectives. At Lammas offer a libation in appreciation for all you have gleaned since the Springtime. There can be some personnel changes in your work place by August 11. August brings important shifts in your career situation. Communicate with colleagues to keep things moving forward. September 1–17 others share their goals and dreams with you. It's a good time to collaborate regarding plans for the future. By the Autumnal Equinox you will find it easy to take charge of situations and it will feel comfortable to assume a leadership role. A competitive, energetic spirit sets the pace throughout October and early November. At Halloween wear either a comfortable sweatshirt or T-shirt with a seasonal motif or message or a chef's outfit. Have a gathering to celebrate the great night of All Hallows. Invite friends to bring a favorite dish. Assemble a buffet of maple, apple, pumpkin and spice and other seasonal desserts for all to share.

Venus is prominent during the last three weeks of November. Your birthday brings extra money and a loving greeting from a special friend. December begins with travel plans and transportation needs accented. You may decide to celebrate the Winter Solstice in a non traditional way or in a different location. Aromatherapy can help to draw in the deep Winter during the shortest of days. Enjoy pine, orange, peppermint and cinnamon fragrances as you embrace the holiday spirit and exude it for others.

January will be all about housing and family dynamics. Selecting new furnishings or adapting to the schedule of a family member can figure into this trend. A fresh coat of paint can do much to freshen a tired room. Starting on January 24 and continuing throughout February family members can be more feisty and argumentative than usual. Offer suggestions for conflict resolution. By Candlemas it will become easier to maintain harmony. Lighting blue and green taper candles for peace would be an effective technique to use as a house blessing. During February social connections are very promising. Communicate with those who are close to you. Share plans to take a short journey. Near the New Moon eclipse on February 17 a relationship reaches a deeper level of trust and intimacy. The end of February brings a trip down memory lane. The people and places which were part of your formative years and are still present in your heart and soul are accented. March 6-20 familiars and small animal companions are especially dear to you now. A special cat, dog, bird, etc. reaches out, showing that the little creature is dependent and craves extra love and attention.

HEALTH

Saturn begins a long transit through your health sector this year. Heed early health indications. Keep up with routine health checkups. Mental and physical well-ness can be enhanced by your lifestyle choices. Analyze how heredity factors and past habits are affecting how you feel. Self care and making good choices are instrumental in enjoying a long life with improved health.

LOVE

The eclipses on September 7 and February 17, 2026 promise profound and life changing situations regarding love. A significant relationship can change near those times. It's a year of endings and beginnings regarding love connections. August and November bring good Venus aspects your way, indicating romantic bliss. Avoid getting mired in an addictive, toxic love fueled by jealousy during April.

SPIRITUALITY

On June 11 Jupiter begins a year long passage through your sector of philosophy and spiritual growth. This year brings tremendous potential for heightened spiritual awakening. November and January are significant times in this pattern. Spiritual teachings rooted in the cosmology of foreign cultures can be helpful and uplifting to you. Consider planning a sacred journey—a pilgrimage—to a spiritual site this year.

FINANCE

Shift focus to paying outstanding debts and fulfilling financial obligations and other old financial business. while Pluto is retrograde May 4–October 14. November through January is a very promising time for financial gains. At that time your past efforts and hard work should show the promise of greater financial rewards.

SAGITTARIUS
November 22–December 20
Spring 2025–Spring 2026 for those
born under the sign of the Archer

A mutable Fire sign ruled by Jupiter, independent and goal oriented Sagittarius resists ever being limited or held down in any way. An adventurous explorer of expansive ideas and pursuer of big dreams, you're determined to have a good time all the while. You cherish freedom and wide open spaces. Symbolized by the Centaur, the half human and half animal sign, Sagittarians usually have a special rapport with animals, especially horses and large dogs.

The Springtime begins with Mercury and Venus both supporting reunions and reconciliations with a relative or friend whom you have been out of touch with. An old regret or grudge can be dissolved. The eclipse on March 29 reinforces this change of heart, giving a relationship a fresh start. Attachment deepens. April 1–20 brings attention to your home and heritage. Making your residence more comfortable becomes a priority. Late April–May 9 favors travel. An invitation to a May Day celebration could involve a journey. The remainder of May through June you will be attracted to new ideas and spiritual concepts. Enrollment in an academic program or educational travel would be appealing. The Full Moon in Sagittarius on June 11 highlights the spe-

cifics. At the Summer Solstice a competitive spirit prevails. You might be challenged to play a game which tests your wits and skills.

During July some tension brews, affecting your career sector. Be diplomatic and tolerant if a coworker is difficult. Devote extra time and effort to problem solving. By Lammas others will want to talk over solutions and resolve differences.

August 1–24 brings loving messages from spirit guides. The presence of loved ones who have passed away can be felt in a comforting dream. Examine financial opportunities as the month ends. September 1–21 humanitarian issues come to your attention. You will reflect upon ways to improve the quality of life for others. Political or civic organizations could be the venue for organizing and doing good deeds The lunar eclipse on September 7 can intensify this goal. At the Autumnal Equinox prepare an observance which honors the future and the season to come. Select goals—ask yourself what you really want. October 1–13 brings enjoyable situations and a sense of genuine camaraderie at work. Business combines gracefully with pleasure. A party at work might be planned. The remainder of October promises a change of pace. The mood becomes more introspective. You will feel the need for some quiet time to gather your thoughts and focus on completing a project. Honor ancestors on Halloween. The All Hallows holiday has an especially sacred feeling this year. A deep purple or black cape would be a good costume choice.

November finds Jupiter turning retrograde. Patience and time are needed with developing financial strategies. An investment or business situation might have to be revamped. November 10–30 postpone making major purchases or signing binding contracts. History is repeating itself in your life. Look to the past to find the right guidance for the present and future. Trust your intuition December 1–11. Your own instincts will offer better guidance than the well meaning advice of others. Your birthday brings invitations and numerous greetings. Others show how much they care about you. As the Winter Solstice nears tension will subside and social connections become increasingly happy and upbeat. Meditate on the sunset as the longest of nights begins.

January 1–16 emphasizes security concerns. Enjoy simple pleasures and live within your means. Conversations revolve around business. January 17–31 brings messages and visits from neighbors or family members. Others have worthwhile news to share yet the communication could have a subtle quality. You might have to "read between the lines" to decode what is actually being expressed. February 1–9 neighbors reach out to share ideas. A receptive response from you can lead to a valuable alliance. At Candlemas light an orange candle for friendship. The remainder of February accents family connections and your home. The March 3 lunar eclipse has a powerful impact on your career. You consider changing your job status or your place of employment in March. Stay informed about new developments in your field as the Winter ends.

HEALTH

Mid April–mid June will find you especially sensitive to temperature extremes. Select the appropriate garments and footwear for the weather and your surroundings to optimize wellness. November 11–March 11 Jupiter's influence favors paying attention to nutrition, weight and diet. Choose healthy foods and drinks then. Also remember to check your weight regularly. Keep it in the correct range during the Autumn and Winter.

LOVE

The eclipse on March 29 impacts your sector of pleasure and romance. This promises shifts in relationships this year. There can be unexpected connections or partings. Mid October–early November brings an especially promising time for love. March 7–18 also indicates blissful romance.

SPIRITUALITY

Neptune, which connects to spiritual influences, is starting a rare sign change this year. For you March 20–October 21 will bring spiritual awakening through music, art and creative expression. Include spiritual motifs in personal creative projects. Design a mandala to illustrate your moods and intuition. Light a fire. Fuel it with fragrant woods and dried leaves. Gaze into the flames and meditate.

FINANCE

From the Vernal Equinox until early June a Jupiter opposition indicates that advice from another might be unwise. Try not to lend or borrow money or risk security in the Springtime. December favors monetary gain. Consider pursuing new financial transactions and promising ventures. Settle debts by December 31.

CAPRICORN
December 22–January 19
Spring 2025–Spring 2026 for those
born under the sign of the Goat

This cardinal sign of Earth is ruled by frosty and solemn Saturn. Structured and hardworking, you are the Zodiac's purposeful planner. However, you also have a caring and charitable side. Others look to you for solutions intimes of trouble. You will gladly share your experiences and offer assistance, especially to the very young and the elderly. Your wry, dry and subtle sense of humor enables you to cope well with life's challenges. Just as your symbol the Goat suggests, you are a climber and a survivor. With determination and persistence you will navigate the mountain scape of life diligently, eventually arriving your destination, the summit.

The Springtime breezes in welcoming a spirit of challenge and heightened energy. A Mars opposition sets the pace March 20–April 17. There can be some rivalry and competition afoot. Make the best of this by projecting good natured enthusiasm. By May Day a favorable Venus aspect takes over. You will win the support of others through careful listening and amicable discussions. During May your sector of home life and heritage is accented. A residential move might be considered. Near the Full Moon on May 12 decorate an altar with potted greenery or a floral arrangement. Mid

May favors landscape design. Consider growing some kitchen herbs or other edible plants.

By June Saturn begins a long term square to your Sun. Your vitality can be variable. Get some extra rest. The last half of June brings upbeat social prospects. Circulate. Accept or issue invitations. Near the Summer Solstice on June 21 attune to tender feelings. Try using affirmations and visualizations to reinforce true love. Late June through July your thoughts will turn toward health and fitness. Include a spa stay, yoga classes or a stroll along a scenic trail in your vacation plans. By Lammas you will enjoy renewed vitality. August brings recognition to a partner. Offer congratulations and share in the happiness. This good news could involve either your coworker or a close personal relationship. September 1–21 brings an awareness of time passing. You will feel an urge to address schedules and deadlines. By the Autumnal Equinox an adventurous spirit develops. The early weeks of Fall will find travel and imported items appealing. Plans to explore are brewing. A learning experience could be involved. October 1–13 you'll be touched by beauty. A concert, art gallery or display of holiday décor could be the catalyst for this. By October 31 your thoughts will turn toward finances. Budgeting and seeking ways to add to your income will be considered. Include a prosperity affirmation with Halloween observances. November 1-18 helpful information arrives regarding your money situation.

Late November will focus on positive social and business connections. Networking and group affiliations guide you toward realizing goals and dreams. December 1-14 will find you seeking quiet corners in order to enjoy solitary reverie. As the Winter Solstice approaches an urge to become involved in charitable endeavors is strong. You might gather holiday gifts and dinners to distribute to those in need. December 25–January 16 brings rewards and appreciation for your good deeds and past efforts. Your birthday brings an unexpected boon. January 17-31 favors gathering needed supplies and shopping for collectibles and specialty items. At Candlemas light tapers in rich jewel tones to create stability and comfort in your environment. Throughout February old disappointments will fade away, anger and regrets are released. Turbulent events from the past are put to rest. A promise is kept or a debt owed to you is repaid near February 26.

The total eclipse on March 3 brings ideas and information to the forefront which will change your understanding concerning a controversial issue. It's especially important to communicate your outlook regarding this. On March 11 Jupiter completes its retrograde. A blockage, perhaps involving a legal or ethical matter, begins to dissolve. It will be easy to finish old business and plan for the future as the Winter draws to a close.

HEALTH

Saturn begins a sign change between May 26–August 31. This brings hereditary health factors to the forefront. Learning all you can about your family's health history can offer clues about managing your own wellness. During mid February a relative or close friend might develop a health issue and request your assistance in care giving. Set some boundaries if this occurs to avoid an obligation which might eventually become too draining for you.

LOVE

A Uranus influence over the past few years has brought an unstable quality around love connections. Uncertain on again/off again situations might have created some emotional insecurity, putting your heart on a roller coaster ride. This will taper off when Uranus begins a sign change in July and begins to leave your love sector. Earthy outdoor environments such as scenic mountains, beautiful gardens and ancient forests would be excellent places to arrange a romantic stroll or picnic.

SPIRITUALITY

The eclipses on September 21 and March 3 both affect your sector of spirituality and philosophy. New approaches to spiritual understanding can develop then. This might involve joining a meditation group or spiritual circle. Visiting sacred sites near either of those two dates could awaken truly profound spiritual realizations.

FINANCE

Pluto is currently transiting your financial sector. The first hint of this transformative and unsettling trend began in March, 2023. It will set the financial tone for you until 2043. Traditional financial guidelines are being revised. World wide economic trends will mirror your personal financial situation. The most promising financial times for you this year are August–September and late January–early February.

AQUARIUS
January 20–February 18
Spring 2025–Spring 2026 for those
born under the sign of the Water Bearer

This fixed sign of Air is ruled by eclectic and original Uranus. You are an innovator. Exploring the impossible and expanding to embrace the surreal and futuristic, the Water Bearer has been called the only completely human of the zodiac signs. The flowing water actually represents circulation, distributing values and democracy in the purest form. Disrupting the status quo in the quest to find better ways of doing things is your focus. Your outlook is more universal than personal. You will tend to detach from connections or situations which are too confining or which cling.

The Springtime is colored by a sense of fate at work. A quincunx from Mars sets the pace from the Vernal Equinox until April 17. Adapt. Perhaps there are some things which can't be changed, at least for the time being. Information and messages arrive near the eclipse on March 29, bringing valuable insights. April 18–30 brings a resolution to a traffic or transportation issue. Celebrate May Day with seasonal stories and songs. Mid May brings a focus on housing issues and family life. A relative might request advice or assistance. A home maintenance issue can come to light. A competitive spirit builds from late May through early June. Keep

the mood light and good humored and all will be well.

As the Summer Solstice nears alternative health care and fitness programs will intrigue you. On MidSummers Day dedicate a meditation or ritual practice to healing. During July your curiosity is piqued. You will be drawn to dedicate time and thought to research and solving mysteries. A spiritual message from the afterlife could be involved. The end of July brings a favorable Venus influence. Social connections are enjoyable. Issue and accept invitations. At Lammas others are very talkative. Be a good listener, there is an interesting tale or bit of news you wouldn't want to miss. The Full Moon in Aquarius on August 9 highlights the specifics. Those who have been expressing confusion and contradictions in early August suddenly find a renewed sense of direction after August 11. The last half of the month favors travel, especially to destinations which offer an interesting history or spiritual tradition.

September accents finances. Early in the month your source of earned income might change. Careful budgeting is the key to managing changes or transitions linked to cash flow. Avoid lending money during the 2nd and 3rd weeks of September. Instead offer encouragement and advice to those who seek your help. As the Autumnal Equinox nears money will be the focus. Late September–October 4 educational interests will captivate you. Enroll in a class or visit a book store to check out the latest publications. Mid October emphasizes career aspirations. A dynamic colleague sets a competitive pace. At Halloween arranging a group ritual dedicated to sending healing and protection to troubled places or people would be fulfilling. For a costume select a wandering Witch or wizard's garb. Include a cape, hat and a walking stick.

November 1–18 expect a busy, rather hectic pace. Multi-tasking is the key to accomplishing everything needed. An ongoing financial issue is resolved after November 28 when Saturn turns direct in your money sector. December 1–22 brings a pleasant influence from Venus. Especially upbeat holiday greetings and invitations arrive. At the Winter Solstice enjoy a favorite holiday film or theatrical production with a small, congenial group. Cherish peace and privacy during late December. You will be ready for rest and reverie. Early January brings charitable endeavors. You will want to share resources and talents dedicated to humanitarian projects. January 16–31 travel is likely. Winter sports could be especially appealing. You will feel restless as your birthday approaches. A vague longing for adventure and action is present. At Candlemas light a bright blue taper dedicated to the future. Write a birthday wish list or review your New Years resolutions by candle light. Uranus completes its retrograde on February 3–4. During the rest of February you will move on, realizing that you are leaving behind something which you've outgrown or are tired of.

March finds Jupiter turning direct in your health sector. Your vitality improves. Focus on improving health habits. An ongoing health concern can be resolved after March 11.

Winter's final days favor studying new financial strategies.

HEALTH
Your circulatory system and sensitivity to temperature extremes always have a bearing on your health. Regular stretching exercises and massage sessions can be worthwhile. Jupiter transits your health sector mid-June until Winter's end. This whole time period favors reaching wellness goals.

LOVE
Friendship is always a factor in true love for you. Be certain that your friends are compatible with your love interest and that you like his or her social circle. The planets indicate happiness in love in the early Spring, in July and January 17–February 8.

SPIRITUALITY
Neptune, which always has a strong impact on spirituality, will be hovering on the cusp of your sector of communication and information this year. Spiritual discussion groups, meditation circles and visits to sacred sites can enhance and awaken your spiritual perceptions. A profound spiritual realization is likely January 27–March 19, 2026.

FINANCE
During the early Springtime a favorable Jupiter influence brings good financial opportunities. The eclipses during September of this year profoundly affect your finances. New developments are likely. Be flexible and vigilant regarding managing investments as well as focusing on earning opportunities. Saturn has been creating a challenging situation regarding your finances for the past several years. This will end after February 14.

PISCES
February 19–March 20
Spring 2025–Spring 2026 for those
born under the sign of the Fish

A mutable sign of Water, Pisces is ruled by Neptune. Sensitive, fluid and receptive, the Fish rides waves of emotions that are often hard to express and understand. Subconscious triggers carry you along, drifting away into the dreamy depths of the cosmic universal waters. Idealistic, often shy, Pisces has an imaginative and creative side. Adaptable, you mirror and are influenced by factors in your surroundings. The harsher realities of life can seem overwhelming. Dedicating yourself to a worthwhile cause, such as artistic expression or rescuing those in need, can offer a way to rise above melancholy.

Neptune, your ruler, is starting a rare sign change at the Vernal Equinox. This ignites a sparkle, a fiery touch of the pioneer spirit within. The idea of exploring new places or life views will have great appeal. The eclipse on March 29 reveals the specifics. Venus conjoins your Sun throughout April. Either a love interest from the past might rekindle, or a present relationship moves forward, reaching a new level of happiness. Prepare an altar of seasonal flowers on May Day. Dedicate it to honoring true love. May 1–9 brings insights into financial situations. The remainder of the month is busy with a number of errands and short journeys. June 1–15 an animal companion or loved one would appreciate some tender loving care. The Summer Solstice favors doing healing affirmations and using natural remedies.

Late June throughout July a Mars trend electrifies partnerships of all kinds. There can be a competitive, abrupt mood brewing with you striving to maintain peace and equilibrium. Humor and a dash of tolerance are needed. Dedicate Lammas to invoking a spirit of goodwill and cooperation.

August 2–12 extra time and patience will be needed in tackling the daily grind. A task might require a do over. You will be determined to solve a mystery August 13–31. Spiritual connections are heightened. A message sent by a benevolent spirit from the afterlife offers valuable insights. September 7 and 21 bring eclipses. These impact your 1st and 7th houses, foreshadowing a shift in an alliance. You'll express yourself in new ways while cultivating new interests. It's a time of evolving. Celebrate the Autumnal Equinox by purchasing new garments, expressing the new you. Donate items which no longer serve you. Throughout the remainder of September kindly words and thoughtful actions from others bring you solace and happiness.

October accents your sector of higher learning and adventure. Study a new topic or travel to visit a "bucket list" destination to widen your philosophical perspective. By Halloween you will be moving onward and upward. Plan an informal gathering with friends on October 31. Exchange anecdotes about the past months over mugs of steaming mulled cider. November 1-18 family members discuss ideas and plans. A home repair or a decorating project could be the topic. Late November brings a benevolent Venus trend. Gatherings are congenial. Enjoy a party, a concert or theatrical production.

December revives nostalgic Winter holiday traditions. Handcrafted gifts and greetings would delight loved ones. A Winter Solstice celebration with colleagues, perhaps an office party, highlights the longest of nights. January brings undercurrents of tension in your social circle. Take care not to rush to judgment and take sides too quickly. The New Moon on January 18 brings new insights which can alter your interpretation of a volatile situation. By the end of the month your natural tendency toward empathy will surface. You will help someone who faces a challenge. At Candlemas set silver candles in a circle to dispel negativity. Early February brings an introspective mood. Cherish this calmer, quieter cycle. Dedicate spare time to interpreting dreams or journaling. On February 7 Mercury enters your birth sign where it remains until the end of March. Plans and options are considered. Conversation is lively, others share inspirational ideas. Traveling near your birthday is likely. The eclipse on February 17 reveals much about the direction of your future.

On March 2 Mars enters Pisces, remaining there through the end of Winter. You'll feel motivated and can accomplish much. A position of leadership or a promotion is made available to you.

HEALTH
Your sensitivity allows nuances in the surroundings to affect both your physical and mental health. Avoid places and people who drain you or emit negative vibes. On February 13, 2026 Saturn completes a passage through Pisces which has lasted for almost three years. Health issues which have challenged you during this difficult Saturn transit can be overcome now.

LOVE
Two eclipses this year (on September 21 and March 3) indicate major shifts in a relationship. An ending and/or beginning could be involved. Allow changes which seem meant to be to occur. Then all will be well in the end. Prospects for happiness in love are present April 12–30, throughout August and during the last half of February.

SPIRITUALITY
Neptune, the celestial indicator of spirituality, has been in Pisces for the past 14 years. This year it makes a rare sign change while retrograding back and forth over the Pisces-Aries cusp. You are emerging from a long spiritual awakening and are preparing to pioneer new spiritual insights. A fire ceremony, incense and candles could be the catalyst for this. Near January 26, when Neptune's final entry into Aries begins, your future spiritual direction surfaces.

FINANCE
The Full Moon on October 6 brings clarity to what was a confusing financial picture earlier in the year. Avoid repeating patterns which haven't boded well in the past regarding financial management. The financial picture brightens in January.

Sites of Awe

Cley Hill and Little Cley Hill, Frome, England

WHILE TRAVELING through Somerset, England with a friend, I planned to visit another friend and author—Alan—in Frome. It was our first in-person meeting and I was quite excited to see this admired author in the flesh!

We had a nice cup of tea in a beautiful area of Frome close to the riverside. Following our tea and walk about town, my friend told us about a fairy hill called Cley Hill that was close by in the area and also that there was a smaller hill—Little Cley Hill—which had even stronger vibes. So we set out to find these magical sites.

I'm thinking that we might have some trouble finding the area, as many of the postal codes that our GPS have given us have been a bit off. But after just a small bit of driving, we can see what looks like the hill that Alan told us about. Fortunately, there is a carpark here with room for us. As with most important sites here in the United Kingdom, there is a sign in the carpark that explains a bit of information about the site. This sign talks about the chalk grassland, steep slopes, thin soils, orchids and butterflies. It also talks about the conservation grazing—you see, cattle graze freely on Cley Hill.

The more important information for me is at the bottom of the sign. Here it talks about the ancient landscape where humans have been active for thousands of years. Here we find

Cley Hill

180

Cley Hill from a distance

remains of part of an Iron Age hill fort that was used 2200 years ago and the two barrows at the summit are burial grounds dating back to the Bronze Age, some 4000 years ago.

Hum. Unfortunately, there is nothing about the hill being a fairy hill, but we shall check it out ourselves. It's quite a walk in distance as well as in maneuvering, constantly dodging the "gifts" left by cows every few feet! Well, here is a cattle gate—a good old fashioned farmer's gate meant to be easy enough for people to use, but not workable for sheep or cattle. As we have seen during our visit to the U.K., this handy piece of ingenuity has been used throughout the countryside, in every place where sheep and cattle are not allowed to pass. We seem to be at a place where we could go one of two ways. I'm traveling with a good friend who is suggesting we take the path to the left. After just a few steps, it is now evident that this is the correct way. The path is now more obviously worn down by travel.

It is a healthy walk and I'm enjoying the air and scenery. As I walk further up the hill, the village below becomes clearer and the trees more colorful. This truly is a spectacular view.

Ok, now it is time to make a steeper climb. A tiny bit of deep breathing, one foot ahead of the other and off I go. Wow, I thought the view was good from down there—this is incredible. I'm going to try to take a panoramic photo of this. I'm going to walk over here to see…oh dear, this is a very steep drop. I think I will walk elsewhere. There are so many photo opportunities from this vantage point. I feel quite fortunate. It is always fun to take photos that will remind me of the feeling and energy of a place visited.

Well, here is a nice place to lay down, close my eyes and commune with nature.

Interesting. While I am laying here, I will close my eyes and sing a short fairy tune that I learned almost 50 years ago. It has been a minute or so and I feel like my body is sinking into the hill—all except my feet, which remained on the surface. Fairies—you never know what you will experience and this wasn't expected. Time to get up because I see a tree over there and if I am right, it a hawthorn. I've got to check it out.

It is a hawthorn! Wow, very dark under this old tree compared to the sunny day beyond the tree's outer branches. The ground here seems a little different from the grassy area outside. It is not only sheltered physically from the space beyond its reach, but it also seems sheltered psychically. This space under here feels very quiet but with a huge amount of potential change available. Not sure what to make of it, so I will kindly leave the energy alone and just enjoy the portal-type of space that it has provided for me to experience.

I'll walk around these trees because the hilltop continues over to the North. There is a small path and some folks walking by. Always feels good to smile and nod here when I'm walking on the public land. It somehow doesn't seem that friendly back at home in the parks. There are a lot of walking paths through both public and private properties here.

Ahead of me I see a small, raised area. It appears to be about 20 feet in diameter. A small bit of a climb and I'm here. What a view! Now I can see further to the Northwest where there is a stone-like berm a hundred yards or so away. I'll check it out later. Off to the Northeast I can see Little Cley Hill. Can't wait to get there. Not much of a feeling right here where I'm

Carniverous cows

standing—it's sort of like a very clean tourist photo opportunity spot. I have found that often the top of a hill has the energy affected by the winds of the area. It can almost hide the energy of the land, making it more intense on the ground, but not so evident if you are standing up. Oh well, moving on…

Walking over to the edge of the hill on the northeast side, I see that it is a little steep going down and probably not the way that we will be getting back to the car. Looks like adventure time, so over the hill we go, down a steep path and now at the base of Little Cley Hill. In sight on the hill there are cows—black cows, which we adoringly have nicknamed the "Carnivorous Black Cows of Cley Hill."

My concern was whether or not there was a bull in sight. My friend is beginning to give me a hard time. "Oh, I see a large bull coming down the hill towards us," he said. Oh dear. But after looking around, I realize that my leg is being pulled… again. Interestingly enough, the cows seem to be interested in us and are getting very close—one maybe 10 feet or so away. Remember, they are carnivorous! Or so the tall tale goes.

As we climb the hill, more and more cows seem to be coming over the hill towards our direction. We keep climbing as my friend keeps "seeing" a bull at every turn. He really is giving me a hard time as this is not easy ground to run on and we would not be able to outrun a bull.

The top of this hill seems more magical than Cley Hill did. This place has a bit more of a fairy flavor to it. I'm going to lay down and sing the song again.

Cley Hill, looking toward Little Cley Hill

Wow, quite different this time and my feet sank into the ground as well. Could it be that this time I took off my sneakers first? Yes, that could very well be it. Sneakers or shoes are a symbol of walking on the Earth. Gotta love the magic—it teaches you lessons at every turn. This is a good time to enjoy the view, meditate and commune with the spirits of the land.

My serene meditation is interrupted by a rustling in the bushes nearby. A bull? I don't think we should wait around to see. Best if we head down the hill now. Uncharted territory, with no map or paths, we start down the hill in a southeasterly direction. No path is in sight yet but I don't see how we could be wrong in going in this direction. Now I can see one of the extremely narrow paths that run in circles around the hills. I'm guessing that these are cow paths. They are well worn on the chalk. We follow one, in places needing to go up to the next ring for a moment in order to avoid an obstruction of some type—fallen tree, washed out path, large rock or something of that sort. Along the way, I'm picking up twigs, leaves and pebbles—you know, Witch souvenirs!

The path sort of ends in a very gnarly bunch of trees and shrubs. I'm sure we are still headed in the correct direction. This is an interesting area as well. It has the feeling of being passed through by folks without even much evidence of it. Eventually, after stepping over many branches and enjoying trying to identify plants, we finally come out at the other side where a path begins again. This path takes us through a gate and into a field that is obviously on the side of Cley Hill where the carpark is located. We continue to navigate through the landmine field of cow "gifts." Eventually we come to another gate, followed by a path leading down to the carpark.

I won't forget the Cley Hills, big and small. I will always have fond memories of the hawthorn tree, the fairy experiences and let's not forget the carnivorous black cows!

This was an exciting adventure. Thank you, Alan, for the wonderful suggestion. It turned out to be so much fun that we are going to take you up on your other suggestion. That would be Woden's Barrow, Odin's Barrow, Adam's Grave, Mercury's Temple—four names all identifying the same site!

—ARMAND TABER

The Hawthorn tree

"If you don't have math, you are like a dodo. Mathematics allows you to abstract and to fly."

—Paul Huson

Reviews

The Earth Priest
Alan Richardson
ISBN 979-8325914386
Independent Publisher
$5.72

IF YOU were to compile a list of seminal figures in 20th century occultism, Dion Fortune's name would undoubtedly appear near the top. Her novel *The Sea Priestess* has inspired generations of occultists, Witches, Goddess worshipers and Pagans. In the introduction to *The Earth Priest*, Alan Richardson describes his own experience of finding a copy of *The Sea Priestess* in a library as a teenager. He relates that reading it was a transformational experience for him, saying, "I was never quite the same boy again." He also discusses two key insights into the work that came later in his life: first, that the places described in *The Sea Priestess* are real—although renamed—places of power, and second that the narrator Wilfrid Maxwell is an "alcoholic, a drug addict, a sneering, snobbish, cross-dressing, sister beating mummy's boy," a reality that Anderson states was originally obscured by Fortune's hypnotic prose.

In *The Earth Priest*, Richardson retells the story of the Sea Priestess from the perspective of Daniel Steele, who represents a more grounded and salt-of-the-Earth—but no less obsessive—counterpoint to Fortune's titular priestess.

Richardson also invites the reader to re-explore the landscape of Fortune's book with the names corrected for a clearer sense of where these places are in the physical world.

For those who, like Richardson himself, found *The Sea Priestess* to be a formative, even transformative read, *The Earth Priest* will offer fresh perspective on this important work. For readers who, also like Richardson, found Wilfrid Maxwell's flaws hard to overlook, *The Earth Priest* will offer a new avenue into the text and an opportunity to consider who Vivien Morgan may be in the eyes of a worthier partner. If you have not revisited Fortune's novel in some time, *The Earth Priest* will serve as a welcome refresher on this classic of occult literature. For any reader, *The Earth Priest* is a chance to spend some time in the odd, witty and always insightful world of Alan Richardson.

The Forbidden Knowledge of the Book of Enoch: The Watchers, Nephilim, Fallen Angels, and the End of the World
Harold Roth
ISBN 978-1578638123
Weiser Books
$18.95

EXPLORING one of antiquity's most enigmatic texts, *The Forbidden Knowledge of the Book of Enoch* is both enlightening and engaging. Through thorough research and a captivating writing style, it serves as a valuable resource for scholars and general readers alike who are interested in ancient texts and mythologies. Expertly synthesizing vast amounts of information, Roth crafts a coherent narrative that makes the complexities of the Enochic tradition accessible and engaging.

The book excels in its examination of the historical context, detailed character analysis and exploration of related texts, providing a comprehensive understanding of the Enochic corpus. Roth's meticulous attention to detail and ability to connect the ancient text with broader cultural themes highlight his scholarly rigor. His nuanced interpretations offer a fresh perspective on the *Book of Enoch*, emphasizing its enduring relevance and impact on both ancient and modern thought.

Roth's passion for the subject is evident, making the complex material accessible and engaging. His connection of ancient narratives with contemporary themes ensures the book resonates with both academics and lay readers. By illuminating the intricate weave of folklore, traditions and spiritual doctrines in the Book of Enoch, Roth encourages readers to explore past mysteries and understand their implications for the present and future.

In summary, *The Forbidden Knowledge of the Book of Enoch* is a must-have for anyone interested in the mysteries of ancient religious literature. Harold Roth has created a richly enlightening book, offering a distinctive view into the ancient world and its lasting influence. This book, available in early December 2024, is set to become a cornerstone in the study of Enochic literature and ancient apocalyptic traditions, providing invaluable insights into to these timeless texts.

Claves Intelligentiarum: A Complete Practical Manual of Conjuration of the Planetary Intelligences
David Rankine
ISBN 13: 978-1-915933-68-3
Hadean Press Limited
£16.99

IN HIS SOON to be released *Claves Intelligentiarum: A Complete Practical Manual of Conjuration of the Planetary Intelligences* David Rankine provides a remarkable guide to the art of conjuring planetary intelligences. This comprehensive manual stands out for its practical methodology, making it essential for both newcomers and experienced practitioners of grimoire magic.

The book is methodically structured, offering a step-by-step guide covering all aspects of conjuration. Rankine begins with preparatory steps, emphasizing fasting, purificatory baths and tool consecration. Each step is meticulously detailed, ensuring readers understand the significance and procedures involved, making complex rituals accessible and manageable.

A standout feature of *Claves Intelligentiarum* is its blend of traditional and modern practices. Rankine integrates historical methods with contemporary techniques like visualization during consecrations, enhancing traditional incantations. The section on fragrances showcases Rankine's wisdom, offering alternatives to traditional incense. His suggestion to use oil burners with essential oils is a thoughtful adaptation for those with respiratory concerns, reflecting Rankine's innovative and empathetic approach.

Rankine explores each planetary intelligence in depth, detailing its qualities, attributes and associated rituals. Supported by historical references and insights from various grimoires, his research makes the rituals accessible and relevant to contemporary practitioners. The book's logical, user-friendly structure guides readers through the conjuration process. Rankine's attention to detail ensures practitioners are well prepared and spiritually aligned. Including additional rituals and the optional "license to remain" for house or nature spirits demonstrates his holistic approach and respect for the spiritual ecosystem.

Claves Intelligentiarum stands out for its thoroughness, practical guidance and adaptability. Rankine's dedication to creating a complete and coherent manual is evident, making this book an invaluable resource for anyone interested in planetary intelligence conjuration. The blend of historical wisdom and practical advice ensures that this guide is informative and functional, catering to the needs of modern practitioners while preserving the rich tradition of grimoire magic.

Seiðr Magic; the Norse Tradition of Divination and Trance
Dean Kirkland
ISBN 978-1-64411-944-0
Destiny Books
$19.99

SEIÐR—a recently reconstructed magical practice with roots in ancient Norse texts and archaeology—is not always easy to learn about since a minority of people in Heathen reconstructionist communities take part in it. In *Seiðr Magic*, Dean Kirkland outlines the historical basis for the practice and provides an invaluable guide for the seeker hoping to learn not just about seiðr, but how to go about doing it.

Kirkland opens by explaining why the common characterization of seiðr as Norse Witchcraft is erroneous. He then discusses what information is available about seiðr from historical texts, and makes the argument that seiðr has its basis in ecstatic trance and is more akin to shamanism than to modern Witchcraft, with its roots in ritual magic. He then opens up the thorny question of reconstruction, which necessarily departs from historical praxes to fill in the gaps of what the historical record does not say. Rather than a reckless embrace of unverified personal gnosis, Kirkland carefully balances resurrecting ancient methods with the concerns and practicalities of the modern context.

To do this, Kirkland first addresses the mistrust of seiðr that can color Heathen reconstructionist communities. He goes on to address misconceptions, such as that it is only for women and relies on the use of drums. Most of the text provides instruction in the practical details of seiðr, with chapters on trance, tools, healing, dealing with the dead and other specific techniques. With each one, Kirkland provides context from archaeology and ancient texts along with detailed guidance for practicing that particular aspect of seiðr.

For the Heathen curious about but perhaps uncomfortable with seiðr or the general Pagan with an interest in ancient magic, Kirkland provides a useful guide to seiðr that is informed by both practice and history, alongside an invaluable discussion of the nuances of culture, worldview and reconstruction.

Healing through Sound: Awakening Your Audible Body
Vickie Dodd
979-8888500316
Findhorn Press
$18.99

VICKIE Dodd hooks you right away, opening with a compelling description of her Ozark upbringing, where granny healers were common and "doctoring"—going to see a medical professional—was an indicator of upward mobility. As a child, she "had the nerves," that is to say, she was perceived as being overly sensitive to the point of anxiety—and indeed she was. As she grew older, Dodd learned how to tune out the excess noise of others' moods and tune in to her own body, to heal her nervous system by teaching herself to listen to the messages of her body and translate these instinctively into sound. In addition to internal perceptions, her teachers were plants, trees, rocks and rivers. She also began to work with other people, beginning with adding intuitive soundings to massage, and eventually she began teaching how to perceive and heal with the inner ear. In *Healing Through Sound; Awakening Your Audible Body*, Dodd provides guidance for any reader interested in learning how to perceive and respond to the deep wisdom of the body.

Dodd's engaging narrative carries you along as she describes her journey—don't be surprised to find yourself having trouble putting the book down! *Healing Through Sound* is more than her own story, though. The book is structured as a guide to healing yourself and others through listening to and expressing sounds. In each chapter, she outlines the topic and provides instructions, practical advice and exercises, while simultaneously offering anecdotes and remembrances, which are, of course, their own teachers. She begins with listening as the primary form of inner perception, describing for the reader how to become aware of the body's messages and advice—whether your own body or another person's. Subsequent chapters cover humming and other sounds, emptying or releasing the suppressed and unexpressed aspects of your experience and aligning or attuning the body. The entire work centers on the concept that the body has wisdom to share and that listening to it and engaging with the parasympathetic nervous system is a path of healing.

The last two chapters and the epilogue will be of particular interest to readers of *The Witches' Almanac*, covering shadow work, the spiritual experience and power of sound and a discussion of trusting the body as an aspect of the awakening of the divine feminine. With a foreword by noted herbalist Rosemary Gladstar, anyone interested in natural healing and the connection between mind, body, soul and nature will find *Healing Through Sound* an indispensable read.

From a Witch's Mailbox

Pappa can you hear me?

What are the best methods for connecting with and honoring ancestral spirits within Pagan traditions?—Submitted by Jade Roberts

Honoring ancestral spirits involves creating a deep, respectful connection with those who have passed on, acknowledging their ongoing presence and influence in our lives. Begin by setting up an ancestral altar, a sacred space dedicated to your ancestors. This altar can include photographs, heirlooms and personal items that belonged to them, as well as symbols representing your heritage. Light candles and incense to invite their presence and purify the space. Regular offerings of food, drink, flowers and other items your ancestors enjoyed in life can be made, symbolizing nourishment and respect. Speak to your ancestors, sharing your thoughts, worries and joys and listen for their guidance in return. This communication can be enhanced through meditation, prayer and rituals performed in their honor.

Incorporating ancestral veneration into seasonal festivals and Sabbats, such as Samhain, can deepen this connection. Samhain—known as the time when the veil between the worlds is thinnest—is particularly powerful for honoring the dead. During these celebrations, set aside time to remember your ancestors, tell their stories and celebrate their lives. Creating a journal dedicated to your ancestors can also be a meaningful practice. This record can include their stories, family traditions and any messages or signs you receive from them. Engaging in genealogical research can further connect you to your roots, providing a tangible link to your lineage.

Additionally, consider the practice of living in a way that honors your ancestors' values and teachings. This can include upholding family traditions, practicing kindness and embodying the strengths and virtues they cherished. By integrating these practices into your spiritual routine, you create a continuous, living bond with your ancestors, honoring their legacy and keeping their memories alive within your life and spiritual path.

It's as clear as mud

How can one develop and enhance their abilities as a seer, particularly in terms of interpreting visions and dreams accurately?—Submitted by Darius Winters

Developing and enhancing abilities as a seer involves a variety of practices focused on increasing intuition, understanding symbolism and refining interpretative skills. Start by maintaining a dream journal, recording dreams immediately upon waking to capture details and identify patterns and recurring symbols. Regular meditation is crucial for enhancing psychic abilities because it quiets the mind, making it easier to receive and interpret intuitive messages and visions. Visualization exercises, where you imagine detailed scenes, can also sharpen the inner eye, making it easier to see and understand visions when they occur spontaneously.

Engaging with divination tools like tarot cards, runes or scrying mirrors helps bridge the conscious and subconscious mind, offering tangible symbols for interpretation. Regular practice with these tools enhances your ability to discern subtle meanings. Additionally, studying mythology, folklore and various symbol systems provides a rich context for interpreting visions and dreams, as understanding common archetypes and their meanings in different cultures can offer deeper insights into the symbols that appear in your visions. Seek out mentorship or community with other practitioners to share experiences and interpretations, gaining new perspectives and validation. Trust in your intuition, remain open to learning and be patient with your progress. Developing seer abilities is a journey that unfolds over time, enriched by consistent practice and an open, receptive mind.

Ethically convenient!

Can you provide guidance on the ethical considerations and responsibilities of practicing magic, especially when it involves influencing others?—Submitted by Bryan Frost

Practicing magic ethically requires responsibility, especially when influencing others. Ensure your actions align with the principles of harm none and respect free will. Before performing any spell affecting others, consider the consequences and motivations. Avoid manipulating or coercing individuals, as this can lead to

negative outcomes. Conduct divination or meditation to understand the impact of your actions and seek guidance from spiritual guides to ensure your intentions align with the greater good. Reflect on your motivations, ensuring they are positive. Balance personal desires with ethical boundaries, recognizing the interconnectedness of all beings. Educate yourself on ethical practices and seek guidance from experienced practitioners.

Let us hear from you, too

We love to hear from our readers. Letters should be sent with the writer's name (or just first name or initials), address, daytime phone number and e-mail address, if available. Published material may be edited for clarity or length. All letters and e-mails will become the property of The Witches' Almanac Ltd. *and will not be returned. We regret that due to the volume of correspondence we cannot reply to all communications.*

The Witches' Almanac, Ltd.
P.O. Box 25239
Providence, RI 02905-7700
info@TheWitchesAlmanac.com
www.TheWitchesAlmanac.com

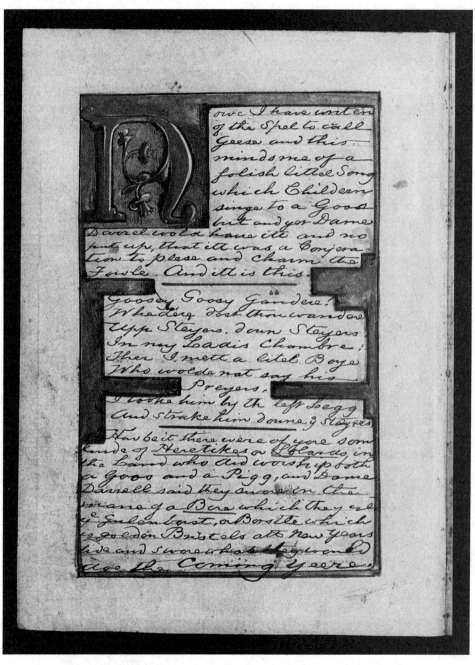

owe I have writen of the Spel to call Geese and this minds me of a folish litel Song which Childern singe to a Goos but and yet Dame Darrel wolde have itt and no put up, that itt was a Conjeration to plese and charm the Fowle. And itt is this.

Goosey Goosy Gandere!
Whe dreg dost thou wandere
Upp Steyers. doun Steyers
In my Ladis Chambre;
Ther I mett a litel Boye
Who wolde nat say his
Preyers.
I tooke him by the left Legg
And strake him doune ý Stayers.

Hau be it there were of yore som kinde of Heretikes or Ilands, in the Land who did worsh up both a Goos and a Pigg, and Dame Darrell said they ware in the mane of a Bore which they cal ý gulen bost, a Borstle which is golden Bristels att New Years tide and swore that they wolde doe the Coming yeere.

Excerpt from

The Witchcraft of Dame Darrel of York

The products and services offered above are paid advertisements.

❧ MARKETPLACE ❧

The products and services offered above are paid advertisements.

❧MARKETPLACE❧

www.AzureGreen.net Jewelry, Amulets, Incense, Oils, Herbs, Candles, Statuary, Gemstones, Ritual Items. Wholesale inquiries welcome.

The Crystal Fox 311 Main Street, Laurel, MD 20707 USA. The largest new age/ metaphysical gift shop in the mid-Atlantic region. Monday-Saturday 10am-9pm Sunday 11am-7pm. **(301) 317-1980,** cryfox@verizon.net, www.TheCrystalFox.biz

The Minoan Brotherhood is a men's initiatory tradition of the Craft celebrating Life, Men Loving Men, and Magic in a primarily Cretan context, also including some Aegean and Ancient Near Eastern mythology—**Minoan-Brotherhood.org**

Coven Work Embark on a transformative journey of traditional lore and ceremonial magick. Experience expert guidance and enriching coven work in Providence, fostering growth and deep spiritual connection. **ProvidenceCoven.org**

The products and services offered above are paid advertisements.

TO: The Witches' Almanac
P.O. Box 1292, Newport, RI 02840-9998
www.TheWitchesAlmanac.com

Email (required) _____

Name_____

Address_____

City_____ State_____ Zip_____

WITCHCRAFT being by nature one of the secretive arts, it may not be as easy to find us next year. If you'd like to make sure we know where you are, why don't you send us your name, email address and street address? You will certainly hear from us.

Aradia
Gospel of the Witches
Charles Godfrey Leland

ARADIA IS THE FIRST work in English in which witchcraft is portrayed as an underground old religion, surviving in secret from ancient Pagan times.

- Used as a core text by many modern Neo-Pagans.
- Foundation material containing traditional witchcraft practices
- This special edition features appreciations by such authors as Paul Huson, Raven Grimassi, Judika Illes, Michael Howard, Christopher Penczak, Myth Woodling, Christina Oakley Harrington, Patricia Della-Piana, Jimahl di Fiosa and Donald Weiser. A beautiful and compelling work, this edition is an up to date format, while keeping the text unchanged. 172 pages $16.95

The ABC of Magic Charms
Elizabeth Pepper

Mankind has sought protection from mysterious forces beyond mortal control. Humans have sought the help of animal, mineral, vegetable. The enlarged edition of *Magic Charms from A to Z*, guides us in calling on these forces. $12.95

The Little Book of Magical Creatures
Elizabeth Pepper and Barbara Stacy

AN UPDATE of the classic *Magical Creatures*, featuring Animals Tame, Animals Wild, Animals Fabulous—plus an added section of enchanting animal myths from other times, other places. *A must for all animal lovers.* $12.95

The Witchcraft of Dame Darrel of York
Charles Godfrey Leland, Introduction by Robert Mathiesen

A beautifully reproduced facsimile of the illuminated manuscript shedding light on the basis for a modern practice. A treasured by those practicing Pagans, as well as scholars.   Standard Hardcover $65.00 or Exclusive full leather bound, numbered and slipcased edition $145.00

DAME FORTUNE'S WHEEL TAROT: A PICTORIAL KEY
Paul Huson

Based upon Paul Huson's research in *Mystical Origins of the Tarot, Dame Fortune's Wheel Tarot* illustrates for the first time the earliest, traditional Tarot card interpretations as collected in the 1700s by Jean-Baptiste Alliette. In addition to detailed descriptions, full color reproductions of Huson's original designs for all 79 cards.

WITCHES ALL

A Treasury from past editions, is a collection from *The Witches' Almanac* publications of the past. Arranged by topics, the book, like the popular almanacs, is thought provoking and often spurs the reader on to a tangent leading to even greater discovery. It's perfect for study or casual reading,

GREEK GODS IN LOVE

Barbara Stacy casts a marvelously original eye on the beloved stories of Greek deities, replete with amorous oddities and escapades. We relish these tales in all their splendor and antic humor, and offer an inspired storyteller's fresh version of the old, old mythical magic.

MAGIC CHARMS FROM A TO Z

A treasury of amulets, talismans, fetishes and other lucky objects compiled by the staff of *The Witches' Almanac*. An invaluable guide for all who respond to the call of mystery and enchantment.

LOVE CHARMS

Love has many forms, many aspects. Ceremonies performed in witchcraft celebrate the joy and the blessings of love. Here is a collection of love charms to use now and ever after.

MAGICAL CREATURES

Mystic tradition grants pride of place to many members of the animal kingdom. Some share our life. Others live wild and free. Still others never lived at all, springing instead from the remarkable power of human imagination.

ANCIENT ROMAN HOLIDAYS

The glory that was Rome awaits you in Barbara Stacy's classic presentation of a festive year in Pagan times. Here are the gods and goddesses as the Romans conceived them, accompanied by the annual rites performed in their worship. Scholarly, lighthearted – a rare combination.

CELTIC TREE MAGIC

Robert Graves in *The White Goddess* writes of the significance of trees in the old Celtic lore. *Celtic Tree Magic* is an investigation of the sacred trees in the remarkable Beth-Luis-Nion alphabet and their role in folklore, poetry and mysticism.

MOON LORE

As both the largest and the brightest object in the night sky, and the only one to appear in phases, the Moon has been a rich source of myth for as long as there have been mythmakers.

MAGIC SPELLS
AND INCANTATIONS

Words have magic power. Their sound, spoken or sung, has ever been a part of mystic ritual. From ancient Egypt to the present, those who practice the art of enchantment have drawn inspiration from a treasury of thoughts and themes passed down through the ages.

LOVE FEASTS

Creating meals to share with the one you love can be a sacred ceremony in itself. With the Witch in mind, culinary adept Christine Fox offers magical menus and recipes for every month in the year.

RANDOM RECOLLECTIONS
III, IV

Pages culled from the original (no longer available) issues of *The Witches' Almanac,* published annually throughout the 1970s, are now available in a series of tasteful booklets. A treasure for those who missed us the first time around, keepsakes for those who remember.

Liber Spirituum

BEING A TRUE AND FAITHFUL REPRODUCTION OF
THE GRIMOIRE OF PAUL HUSON

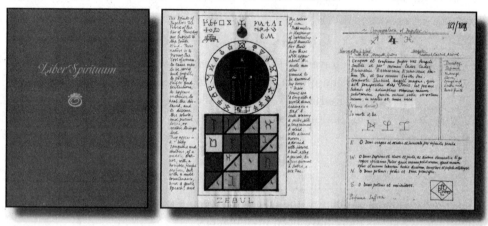

In 1966, as an apprentice mage, Paul Huson began the work of constructing his personal *Liber Spirituum* or *Book of Spirits*. The origins of his work in fact have their genesis a number of years before he took up the pen to illuminate the pages of his *Book of Spirits*. It was in his tender youth that Paul's interest in matters magical began. It was his insatiable curiosity and thirst for knowledge that would eventually lead him to knock on the doors of Dion Fortune's Society of the Inner Light in 1964, as well as studying the practices of the Hermetic Order of the Golden Dawn and the Stella Matutina under the aegis of Israel Regardie. Drawing on this wellspring of knowledge and such venerable works as the *Key of Solomon*, *The Magus*, *Heptameron*, *Three Books of Occult Philosophy* as well as others set down a unique and informed set of rituals, in addition to employing his own artistry in the creation of distinctive imagery.

Using the highest quality photographic reproduction and printing methods, Paul's personal grimoire has here been faithfully and accurately reproduced for the first time. In addition to preserving the ink quality and use of gold and silver paint, this facsimile reproduction has maintained all of Huson's corrections, including torn, pasted, missing pages and his hand drawn and renumbered folios. Preserved as well are the unique characteristics of the original grimoire paper as it has aged through the decades. In this way, the publisher has stayed true to Paul Huson's *Book of Spirits* as it was originally drawn and painted.

223 Pages
Paperback — $59.95
Hardbound in slipcase — $149.95

For further imformation visit: TheWitchesAlmanac.com

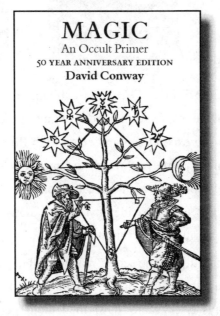

Ancient Holidays Series

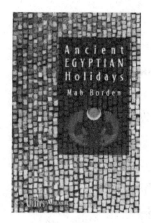  

INTRODUCING ANCIENT HOLIDAYS, an exhilarating new book series that immerses readers into the captivating world of ancient civilizations' spiritual calendars. Authored by the exceptionally talented Mab Borden, these books offer profound and enlightening journeys through the sacred calendars of the ancient Egyptians, Greeks, and Romans. With great excitement, we present this series, confident that it will not only provide invaluable knowledge but also kindle inspiration for our own spiritual observations.

Within each captivating title of the series, readers will delve into comprehensive explanations of the months and seasons, gaining profound insights into the significance of sacred days. Every sacred day is meticulously detailed, encompassing the deity being honored and the social and ritual activities associated with it. Additionally, each publication is enriched with information-packed appendices, which provide a wealth of knowledge, including the mapping of deity holidays to the corresponding seasons.

For futher details and to order visit us at:
TheWitchesAlmanac.com/pages/the-ancient-holiday-series

ORDER FORM

Each timeless edition of *The Witches' Almanac* is unique.
Limited numbers of previous years' editions are available.

Item	Price	Qty.	Total
2025-2026 The Witches' Almanac – Air: Breath of the Cosmos			
2024-2025 The Witches' Almanac – Fire: Forging Freedom	$13.95		
2023-2024 The Witches' Almanac – Earth: Origin of Chthonic Powers	$13.95		
2022-2023 The Witches' Almanac – The Moon: Transforming the Inner Spirit	$12.95		
2021-2022 The Witches' Almanac – The Sun: Rays of Hope	$12.95		
2020-2021 The Witches' Almanac – Stones: The Foundation of Earth	$12.95		
2019-2020 The Witches' Almanac – Animals: Friends & Familiars	$12.95		
2018-2019 The Witches' Almanac – The Magic of Plants	$12.95		
2017-2018 The Witches' Almanac – Water: Our Primal Source	$12.95		
2016-2017 The Witches' Almanac – Air: the Breath of Life	$12.95		
2014-2015 The Witches' Almanac – Mystic Earth	$12.95		
2013-2014 The Witches' Almanac – Wisdom of the Moon	$11.95		
2012-2013 The Witches' Almanac – Radiance of the Sun	$11.95		
2011-2012 The Witches' Almanac – Stones, Powers of Earth	$11.95		
2010-2011 The Witches' Almanac – Animals Great & Small	$11.95		
2009-2010 The Witches' Almanac – Plants & Healing Herbs	$11.95		
2008-2009 The Witches' Almanac – Divination & Prophecy	$10.95		
2007-2008 The Witches' Almanac – The Element of Water	$9.95		
1993-2006 issues of The Witches' Almanac	$10.00		
The Witches' Almanac 50 Year Anniversary Edition, paperback	$15.95		
The Witches' Almanac 50 Year Anniversary Edition, hardbound	$24.95		
2023-2024 The Witches' Almanac Wall Calendar	$14.95		
SALE: Bundle I—8 Almanac back issues (1991, 1993–1999)	$50.00		
Bundle II—10 Almanac back issues (2000–2009)	$65.00		
Bundle III—10 Almanac back issues (2010–2019)	$100.00		
Bundle IV—30 Almanac back issues (1993–2022)	$199.00		
Ancient Egyptian Holidays	$16.95		
Ancient Greek Holidays	$18.95		
Ancient Roman Holidays	$19.95		
Liber Spirituum—The Grimoire of Paul Huson, paperback	$59.95		
Liber Spirituum—The Grimoire of Paul Huson, hardbound in slipcase	$149.95		
Dame Fortune's Wheel Tarot: A Pictorial Key	$19.95		
Magic: An Occult Primer—50 Year Anniversary Edition, paperback	$24.95		
Magic: An Occult Primer—50 Year Anniversary Edition, hardbound	$29.95		
The Witches' Almanac Coloring Book	$12.00		
The Witchcraft of Dame Darrel of York, clothbound, signed and numbered, in slip case	$85.00		
The Witchcraft of Dame Darrel of York, leatherbound, signed and numbered, in slip case	$145.00		
Aradia or The Gospel of the Witches	$16.95		
The Horned Shepherd	$16.95		

Item	Price	Qty.	Total
The ABC of Magic Charms	$12.95		
The Little Book of Magical Creatures	$12.95		
Greek Gods in Love	$15.95		
Witches All	$13.95		
Ancient Roman Holidays (original first printing)	$9.95		
Celtic Tree Magic	$9.95		
Love Charms	$9.95		
Love Feasts	$9.95		
Magic Charms from A to Z	$12.95		
Magical Creatures	$12.95		
Magic Spells and Incantations	$12.95		
Moon Lore	$9.95		
Random Recollections Volumes III and IV	$9.95		
The Rede of the Wiccae – Hardcover	$49.95		
The Rede of the Wiccae – Softcover	$22.95		
Keepers of the Flame	$20.95		
Sounds of Infinity	$24.95		
The Magic of Herbs	$24.95		
Harry M. Hyatt's Works on Hoodoo and Folklore: A Full Reprint in 13 Volumes (including audio download) *Hoodoo—Conjuration—Witchcraft—Rootwork*	$1,400.00		
Single volumes are also available starting at	$120.00		
Subtotal			
Tax *(7% sales tax for RI customers)*			
Shipping & Handling *(See shipping rates section)*			
TOTAL			

MISCELLANY			
Item	**Price**	**QTY.**	**Total**
Sterling Silver Colophon	$35.00		
Pouch	$3.95		
Skull Scarf	$20.00		
Hooded Sweatshirt, Blk	$30.00		
Hooded Sweatshirt, Red	$30.00		
L-Sleeve T, Black	$15.00		
L-Sleeve T, Red	$15.00		
S-Sleeve T, Black/W	$15.00		
S-Sleeve T, Black/R	$15.00		

MISCELLANY			
Item	**Price**	**QTY.**	**Total**
S-Sleeve T, Dk H/R	$15.00		
S-Sleeve T, Dk H/W	$15.00		
S-Sleeve T, Red/B	$15.00		
S-Sleeve T, Ash/R	$15.00		
S-Sleeve T, Purple/W	$15.00		
Magnets – set of 3	$1.50		
Subtotal			
Tax (7% for RI Customers)			
Shipping and Handling (call for estimate)			
Total			

Payment available by check or money order payable in U.S. funds or credit card or PayPal

The Witches' Almanac, Ltd., PO Box 25239, Providence, RI 02905-7700

(401) 847-3388 (phone) • (888) 897-3388 (fax)
Email: info@TheWitchesAlmanac.com • www.TheWitchesAlmanac.com